THE CALIFORNIA DIRECTORY OF

FINE WINERIES

CENTRAL COAST

THE CALIFORNIA DIRECTORY OF
FINE WINERIES

K. REKA BADGER AND CHERYL CRABTREE, WRITERS

ROBERT HOLMES, PHOTOGRAPHER

TOM SILBERKLEIT, EDITOR AND PUBLISHER

WINE HOUSE PRESS

CONTENTS

INTRODUCTION

Navigating California's burgeoning Central Coast wine country can be intimidating. Hundreds of wineries—from enchanting estates to storefront tasting rooms, from nationally recognized labels to hidden gems—can be found throughout the counties of Santa Barbara and San Luis Obispo. They are waiting to be discovered. The challenge is in deciding where to go and how to plan a trip. This book will be your indispensable traveling companion.

The fifty-eight wineries in the Central Coast edition of *The California Directory of Fine Wineries* are known for producing some of the region's most admired wines. From the moment you walk into these wineries and tasting rooms, you will be invited to converse and sample at a leisurely tempo. In this down-to-earth wine country, passionate vineyard owners and winemakers enjoy experimenting and strive to make distinctive wines that please themselves as well as their devoted customers. Whether you are a novice wine taster or a longtime connoisseur, I suggest that you try unfamiliar wines. You'll be rewarded with outstanding blends and local specialties often unavailable elsewhere.

Although the quality of the winemaker's art is of paramount importance, the wineries are also notable as tourist destinations. Many feature distinctive contemporary architecture. Others are housed in meticulously preserved historic structures. Some host food-and-wine pairings, barrel tastings, art exhibits, concerts, grape stomps, and weekend barbecues. You will also enjoy taking informative behind-the-scenes tours, strolling through colorful gardens, and picnicking on the edge of the vineyards.

As you explore this region, you'll encounter some of California's most appealing scenery and attractions—mountain ranges, dramatic coastline, abundant parkland, and historic towns. Use the information in this book to plan your trip, and be sure to stop along the way to take in the sights. You have my promise that traveling to your destination will be as pleasurable as the wine tasted upon your welcome.

—Tom Silberkleit
Editor and Publisher
Wine House Press
Sonoma, California

What Is an Appellation?

Winemakers often showcase the source of their fruit by citing an *appellation*, a word that refers to the geographical area where wine grapes were grown. An appellation is a specific growing region that, in the United States, is usually determined by borders such as state and county lines, rather than by geography. When an appellation, such as Edna Valley or Santa Rita Hills, appears on a wine label, it indicates that at least 85 percent of the fruit for the wine came from that area.

Although frequently used interchangeably, the terms "appellation of origin" and "American Viticultural Area" (AVA) are not synonymous. AVAs, in contrast to appellations, are defined by natural features: soil types, climate, and topography such as rivers and mountain ranges. The U.S. Alcohol and Tobacco Tax and Trade Bureau defines the characteristics of an AVA and has the authority to approve or deny applications for new AVAs. When wineries or other interested parties want to create an AVA, they must submit documented research to the bureau proving that the area has enough specific attributes to distinguish it significantly from surrounding areas.

Winemakers know that identifying the origin of the grapes can lend prestige to a wine, particularly if the appellation has earned a reputation for high quality. It also provides valuable information about what's inside the bottle. For instance, a Pinot Noir from the hundred-square-mile Santa Rita Hills appellation is likely to vary from one sourced from the more generic California appellation, which includes grapes from all over the state. Moreover, informed consumers and wine connoisseurs know that a Chardonnay from the Santa Maria Valley, for instance, is apt to have a different aroma and taste from a Chardonnay originating in Paso Robles.

When a winery located in one appellation uses grapes from another appellation to make a particular wine, the label indicates the source of the fruit, rather than the physical location of the winery. For example, Ortman Family Vineyards, in the Paso Robles appellation, sources Chardonnay from Edna Valley. Hence the label reads "Ortman Family Vineyards Chardonnay, Edna Valley."

Santa Barbara and San Luis Obispo counties currently contain or are located within the following appellations:

Santa Barbara County

Central Coast
Happy Canyon (proposed viticultural area)
Santa Maria Bench (proposed viticultural area)
Santa Maria Valley
Santa Ynez Valley
Sta. Rita Hills
Yountville

San Luis Obispo County

Arroyo Grande Valley
Central Coast
Edna Valley
Paso Robles
York Mountain

THE MAKING OF WINE

Most vintners agree that wine is made not in the cellar, but in the vineyard, where sun, soil, and water—collectively known as *terroir*—impart varietal flavor. Growers select vineyard sites for many reasons, including exposure and low fertility, for lean soils often produce the most flavorful fruit. Based on the *terroir*, they plant varietals and clones (also called subvarietals) that will grow best, and then wait three years or more for the vines to mature before ever picking a grape.

Harvest brings intense activity, as truckloads of ripe grapes roll into the winery, ready to be crushed and destemmed. After crush, white grapes are pressed, and their juice sent to barrels or stainless steel tanks for fermentation, while red grapes are held for a short time—skins and all—to extract color and flavor before fermentation. Winemakers introduce commercially grown yeast or rely on ambient wild yeast to trigger fermentation, a roiling process during which yeast converts grape sugar into alcohol and carbon dioxide. Fermentation stops when the yeast runs out of sugar, which results in a dry wine. Or, the winemaker quickly chills the wine, killing the yeast and leaving behind a little residual sugar for sweetness.

After fermentation, most wines spend from a few months to a year or more in oak barrels to develop complexity and absorb hints of the toasted interior of the barrel itself. Red wines usually rest in the barrel longer than whites. Most rosés and crisp white wines, such as Johannisburg Riesling, spend little or no time in the barrel.

Throughout the process, winemakers taste their young wares, checking for signs of spoilage and imbalance. They analyze samples in a laboratory to determine the chemical makeup of the wine, which helps them to correct potential problems and maintain stability as the wines continue to evolve. Prior to bottling, vintners spend hours tasting wine from tanks and barrels to come up with optimum combinations for their final blends. Once in the bottle, rosés and light, fruity whites are usually released quickly. Robust reds remain at the winery for several months to a year or so, which gives them a chance to mature and soften before their release.

To make sparkling wine using the *méthode champenoise*, vintners combine a blended base wine—usually Chardonnay or Pinot Noir fermented without the skins—with sugar and yeast. The mixture goes into heavy glass bottles, where a secondary fermentation takes place, giving the wine its signature bubbles. The wine ages for a year or more, and then dead yeast cells are removed in a process called disgorging, a little wine is added back to the bottle, and a natural cork wired in place.

Wine lovers often buy several bottles of a favorite vintage and store them in a cellar or cool closet. That way, they can open a bottle every year or so, and enjoy the subtle flavor shifts as the wine continues to mature over time.

READING A WINE LABEL

When you encounter an unfamiliar bottle of wine, you can learn a lot about it from inspecting the label. Federal law requires wineries to print specific information on the front label of each bottle. Some wineries include details on how a wine was made or how well it will pair with specific foods, usually on a separate label on the back of the bottle.

Most prominently displayed on the label is the name of the winery or the brand name. Also given emphasis is the type of wine. In most cases, this is the grape varietal, such as Chardonnay or Zinfandel. To carry the name of a varietal, the wine must be made of 75 percent of that varietal. Wineries can also use a generic name or a proprietary one such as Tablas Creek Vineyard's Esprit de Beaucastel.

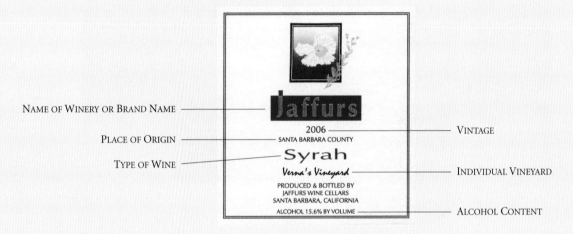

The place of origin on the label tells you where the grapes were grown, not necessarily where the wine was made. A label bearing the name "California" means that 100 percent of the grapes were grown within the state. To use a county name, 75 percent of the grapes must come from that county. To use an American Viticultural Area (AVA) or appellation, at least 85 percent of the grapes must come from the defined area. The vintage is the year the grapes were harvested, not the year the wine was released. The wine must contain at least 95 percent of the stated vintage. Labels sometimes identify an individual vineyard. This is a way for the winemaker to indicate that the grapes came from an exceptional source. To be a vineyard-designated wine, a minimum of 95 percent of the grapes must have come from the vineyard named. Any wine with an alcohol content of more than 14 percent must carry this information. Wines designated as "table wine," with 7 to 14 percent alcohol content, are not required to state such information. American-made wine that contains sulfites must say so on the front or back label. Sulfur dioxide is a natural by-product of winemaking. Some wineries also add sulfites as a preservative.

Other information found on labels may include the description "estate bottled." This tells you that the winery owns (or controls) the vineyard where the grapes were grown and that both the winery and the vineyard are in the same AVA. A bottle labeled "reserve" indicates that the wine is of a superior quality compared with the winery's nonreserve offerings.

Labels for sparkling wines may contain the term *méthode champenoise*. The most salient feature of this process is allowing the wine to ferment for a second time inside the bottle, resulting in bubbles that are finer than those in sparkling wine made by other methods. Vintage sparkling wines are designated as either regular vintage or *prestige cuvée* (also called *tête de cuvée* or premium vintage), meaning that the wine is the top of the line.

THE ETIQUETTE OF WINE TASTING

Most of the wineries profiled in this book offer amenities ranging from inviting gardens to winemaker dinners, but their main attraction is the tasting room. This is where winery employees get a chance to share their products and knowledge with consumers, in hopes of establishing a lifelong relationship. They are there to please.

Yet, for some visitors, the ritual of tasting fine wines can be intimidating. Perhaps it's because swirling wine and using a spit bucket seem to be unnatural acts. But with a few tips, even a first-time taster can enjoy the experience.

After all, the point of tasting is to enhance your knowledge by learning the differences among varieties of wines, styles of winemaking, and appellations. A list of available wines is usually posted, beginning with whites and ending with the heaviest reds or, if available, dessert wines. Look for the tasting notes, which are typically set out on the counter; refer to them as you taste each wine.

After you are served, hold the stem of the glass with your thumb and as many fingers as you need to maintain control. Lift the glass up to the light and note the color and intensity of the wine. Good wines tend to be bright, with the color fading near the rim. Next, gently swirl the wine in the glass. Observe how much of the wine adheres to the sides of the glass. If lines—called legs—are visible, the wine is viscous, indicating body or weight as well as a high alcohol content. Now, tip the glass to about a 45-degree angle, take a short sniff, and concentrate on the aromas. Swirl the wine again to aerate it, releasing additional aromas. Take another sniff and see if the "bouquet" reminds you of anything— rose petals, citrus fruit, or a freshly ironed pillowcase, for example—that will help you identify the aroma.

Finally, take a sip and swirl the wine around your tongue, letting your taste buds pick up all the flavors. The wine may remind you of honey or cherries or mint—as with the "nosing," try to make as many associations as you can. Then spit the wine into the bucket on the counter. Afterward, notice how long the flavor stays in your mouth; a long finish is the ideal. If you don't want another taste, just pour the wine remaining in your glass into the bucket and move on. Remember, the more you spit or pour out, the more wines you can sample.

The next level of wine tasting involves guided tastings and food-and-wine pairings. In these sessions, a few cheeses or appetizers are paired with a flight of wines, usually a selection of three red or three white wines presented in the recommended order of tasting. The server will explain what goes with what.

If you still feel self-conscious, practice at home. Once you are in a real tasting room, you'll be better able to focus on the wine itself. That's the real payoff, because once you learn what you like and why you like it, you'll be able to recognize wines in a similar vein anywhere in the world.

SANTA
BARBARA
COUNTY

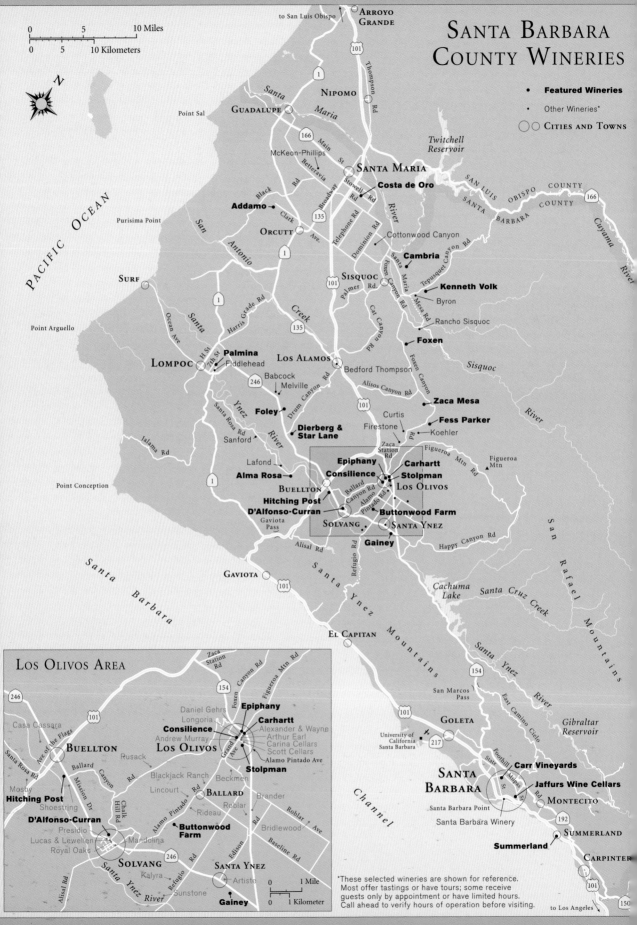

One of the world's extraordinary geographic anomalies defines Santa Barbara County wine country. Rather than being oriented north-south, the mountain ranges run east-west. The towering peaks and sloping hillsides funnel cool winds and fog from the Pacific Ocean through river valleys, resulting in an incredible geographic diversity and a superior environment for growing premium wine grapes. Until the late 1960s, only a handful of vineyards existed here. After University of California scientific research pointed to the area's potential  as a premier wine-grape region, pioneering vintners planted vines with little other than instinct to guide them. Their experiences and successes—especially with award-winning Pinot Noir and Chardonnay—helped put Santa Barbara County on the international wine map. Today the county boasts more than twenty-three thousand acres of vineyards. Of the county's many wineries, more than half produce fewer than two thousand cases a year.

Vineyards, interspersed with organic farms, thoroughbred horse ranches, and cattle ranches, blanket the rural landscape north of the Santa Ynez Mountains. Two-lane roads connect the small Danish-themed town of Solvang with the Old West villages of Los Olivos and Santa Ynez, and picturesque Highway 246 winds westward through Buellton and the Santa Rita Hills to the westernmost city of Lompoc. The vast Los Padres National Forest bounds the eastern sectors. On the south side, the wild beaches of the rugged Gaviota coast stretch forty miles to the vibrant city of Santa Barbara.

ADDAMO ESTATE VINEYARDS

Home-style bistro food goes hand in hand with fine wines and family fun at the lively Addamo Estate Vineyards tasting room in sleepy Old Town Orcutt, a former stagecoach stop in northwest Santa Barbara County. David Addamo was raised in a farming family of Sicilian descent. When he met Liz in the 1990s, he was growing walnuts and apricots in Hollister. Liz, a professional chef, owned a steak house. After they married, they pondered business ventures that would meld their worlds. Dave had helped his amateur-winemaker parents farm their Cabernet Sauvignon vineyard in Hollister, and they inspired him to grow grapes and produce his own wines. Liz agreed that pairing estate wines with opportunities for her creative cooking held great promise. After searching for a Central Coast location ideal for Pinot Noir and Chardonnay, they purchased property just ten miles from the Pacific Ocean and a cooling maritime influence that would lengthen the grapes' hang time and promote deep, complex flavors. In 2000 the Addamos planted six varietals, including Pinot Noir, Chardonnay, Syrah, and Grenache.

The Addamos released their first wines, crafted at a private facility in nearby Santa Maria, in 2005. That same year they opened the contemporary Tuscan-style tasting room and bistro. Both the wines and the tasting room quickly achieved stardom: Addamo Estate Pinot Noir, Chardonnay, and other vintages received national recognition, and the tasting room became one of the area's most popular wine-and-dine destinations.

Guests at the tasting room can taste flights of Addamo wines. Nearly everyone complements the wine samples with orders from the bistro menu, which offers such comfort foods as salads tossed with vinaigrettes made from estate wines, blue cheese biscuits and cheese bread, homemade lasagna, and pizzas. Kids and adults doodle with crayons on paper place mats, while piped-in music enlivens the atmosphere. A mural of the Addamo family estate home and sustainably farmed vineyards—along with a rendering of the winery in progress down the road—overlooks tables in a separate dining alcove.

The relatively new winery has many plans in the works. The Addamos hired Justin Mund, a young rising star already attracting critical acclaim for stellar Pinot Noir production, as director of winemaking. The couple also recently broke ground on a winery complex at the estate vineyards just four miles to the east. The thirty-eight-thousand-square-foot center—yet another marriage of food, fine wine, and lively entertainment—will include a state-of-the-art winery, a tasting room, caves, an event center, and a bakery and deli.

ADDAMO ESTATE VINEYARDS
400 East Clark Ave.
Orcutt, CA 93455
805-937-6400
info@addamovineyards.com
www.addamovineyards.com

OWNERS: David and Liz Addamo.

LOCATION: 6 miles south of downtown Santa Maria.

APPELLATION: Santa Maria Valley.

HOURS: 11 A.M.–9 P.M. Tuesday–Friday; 11 A.M.– 7 P.M. Saturday and Sunday.

TASTINGS: $10 for 6 wines. Barrel tasting by apppointment.

TOURS: None.

THE WINES: Cabernet Sauvignon, Chardonnay, Dolcetto, Grenache, Merlot, Nebbiolo, Pinot Grigio, Pinot Noir, port, Riesling, Rosé, Sangiovese, Syrah.

SPECIALTIES: Chardonnay, Pinot Noir, Syrah.

WINEMAKER: Justin Mund.

ANNUAL PRODUCTION: 7,000 cases.

OF SPECIAL NOTE: Combined tasting room and bistro restaurant. Packed lunches available Thursday–Sunday. Bimonthly food-and-wine pairings. Gift shop with crafts, baskets, and gourmet foods.

NEARBY ATTRACTIONS: Santa Maria Museum of Flight; Rancho Guadalupe Dunes Preserve (fishing, hiking, bicycling, bird-watching).

ALMA ROSA WINERY & VINEYARDS

ALMA ROSA WINERY & VINEYARDS
7250 Santa Rosa Rd.
Buellton, CA 93427
805-688-9090
info@almarosawinery.com
www.almarosawinery.com

OWNERS: Richard and Thekla Sanford.

LOCATION: 5 miles west of U.S. 101 via Santa Rosa Rd. exit.

APPELLATION: Sta. Rita Hills.

HOURS: 11 A.M.–4:30 P.M. daily.

TASTINGS: $10 for 6 wines. Reservations required for groups of 8 or more.

TOURS: None.

THE WINES: Chardonnay, Pinot Blanc, Pinot Gris, Pinot Noir, Pinot Noir Vin Gris.

SPECIALTIES: Chardonnay, Pinot Noir.

WINEMAKER: Christian Roguenant.

ANNUAL PRODUCTION: 20,000 cases.

OF SPECIAL NOTE: Beautiful setting with creekside picnic area. Wildlife identification guides provided for visitor use in tasting room. Special premium bottlings available in tasting room.

NEARBY ATTRACTIONS: Historic Mission La Purísima; Nojoqui Falls County Park (hiking trails, picnic areas near seasonal waterfall).

In the late 1960s, UC Berkeley geography graduate Richard Sanford returned from service in Vietnam yearning for a career far removed from the sadness of war. The prospect of growing Pinot Noir grapes intrigued him, and he embarked on a study of California climate data collected since 1900. The statistics revealed fascinating patterns in northern Santa Barbara County, where the unusual transverse mountain range runs east-west, funneling cool maritime air through the valleys to moderate the growing climate. Sanford was convinced that this part of the state could produce world-class Pinot Noir grapes to rival the best in France.

Sanford drove up and down the roads in the hills and valleys near Lompoc with an agricultural thermometer attached to his windshield and discovered temperature variations ideal for Pinot Noir in the Santa Rita Hills, where grape  growing was virtually unheard of at the time. In 1970 he cofounded the region's first Pinot Noir vineyard, Sanford & Benedict. In 1981 Sanford and his wife, Thekla, started Sanford Winery and a year later purchased the seven-hundred-acre Rancho El Jabalí (Ranch of the Wild Boar), part of the original mid-1800s Rancho Santa Rosa Mexican land grant. They planted the county's first certified organic vineyards and made balanced, elegant wines that garnered widespread international acclaim and helped establish Santa Rita Hills as an official appellation.

In 2005 the Sanfords separated from their namesake winery and began a new venture dedicated to organic farming and sustainable business practices, retaining Rancho El Jabalí, the tasting room, and a hundred-plus acres of certified organic vineyards. In Spanish, *alma* means "soul," and the name Alma Rosa embodies the Sanfords' philosophy that their wines reflect the soul of the historic rancho. Winemaker Christian Roguenant focuses on continuing the Sanfords' reputation for excellence in Pinot Noir and Chardonnay, as well as small quantities of Pinot Gris, Pinot Blanc, and Pinot Noir Vin Gris, a dry rosé.

At El Jabalí, visitors can spot many species of birds and other wildlife. The long, gravel driveway winds through vineyards and sycamore groves, over a creek, up to the rustic tasting room—a converted tin-roofed 1920s dairy barn fashioned from pine planks. A pine tasting bar and cabinetry, red Spanish tile floor, original art by the Sanfords' friends, and bookcases filled with Richard's extensive collection of books lend the comfortable feeling of a Mexican hacienda to the interior. Outdoors, visitors unwind on the shaded stone patio, surrounded by stone flower boxes, a courtyard fountain, and groves of redwood trees, in sight of picnic tables above the spring-fed creek.

BUTTONWOOD FARM WINERY & VINEYARD

Scenic Alamo Pintado Road wends its way through a bucolic five-mile valley between Solvang and the village of Los Olivos. Buttonwood Farm, a working farm since the 1800s, occupies 106 acres in the heart of the valley. Much of the property remains an undisturbed wildlife ecosystem, and native buttonwood trees, also called sycamores, pepper the landscape. Orchards laden with peaches, pomegranates, pears, olives, and almonds and gardens filled with vegetables, herbs, and flowers surround the cottage-style tasting room visible from the roadside entrance.

Betty Williams, an avid equestrian, purchased Buttonwood Farm in 1968 to build a new home and develop a thoroughbred horse breeding and training facility. Williams felt strongly about preserving the local environment for Santa Barbara County. In the vinced her that the sandy lime- would make an excellent vineyard son-in-law, Bret Davenport, of sustainably farmed Bordeaux 1989 completed a winery next to resident artist, Seyburn Zorthian, studies with an abstract brush-

2007 Sauvignon Blanc
SANTA YNEZ VALLEY
Estate Grown

and cofounded the Land Trust early 1980s a vintner friend con- stone plateau east of the creek site. In 1983 Williams and her started planting thirty-nine acres and Rhône-style grapes, and in the vineyard. Her daughter and created label art influenced by stroke master in Japan.

With award-winning winemaker Mike Brown at the helm, the winery developed steadily from its initial 562-case bottling to its current level. Since 1996, Buttonwood Farm's Sauvignon Blanc has attracted widespread acclaim, and Sauvignon Blanc continues to comprise more than a third of the winery's total production. In the early years Buttonwood Farm sold most of its grapes to other Central Coast winemakers, including Bryan Babcock and Adam Tolmach. After 1998 Buttonwood kept all of its estate fruit for its own wines. Mike Brown left his position to focus on his own label, and Karen Steinwachs became head winemaker in 2007. Steinwachs, who previously assisted Norm Yost when he was at Foley Estates Vineyard & Winery and worked as assistant winemaker to Kathy Joseph at Fiddlehead Cellars, is beginning to experiment with new wines, some from recently planted Grenache, Grenache Blanc, Viognier, and Malbec grapes.

Visitors to the casual, light-filled tasting room can sample recent Buttonwood Farm releases amid colorful floral arrangements—freshly cut from the garden—and displays of gifts and food items, including estate-made peach preserves and tomatillo salsa. Weather permitting, the staff often pours wine on the outdoor patio. Guests are welcome to stroll the shale paths through the rambling gardens and relax in the shade of the buttonwood trees.

BUTTONWOOD FARM WINERY & VINEYARD
1500 Alamo Pintado Rd.
Solvang, CA 93463
805-688-3032
info@buttonwoodwinery.com
www.buttonwoodwinery.com

OWNERS: Bret C. Davenport, Seyburn Zorthian, Barry Zorthian.

LOCATION: 2 miles north of Hwy. 246.

APPELLATION: Santa Ynez Valley.

HOURS: 11 A.M.–5 P.M. daily.

TASTINGS: $10 for 7 wines (includes complimentary wineglass).

TOURS: None.

THE WINES: Cabernet Franc, Cabernet Sauvignon, Cabernet Sauvignon Hawk Red (Cabernet Sauvignon, Cabernet Franc blend), Marsanne, Merlot, Sauvignon Blanc, Semillon, Syrah, Trevin (Cabernet Sauvignon, Merlot, Cabernet Franc blend).

SPECIALTY: Sauvignon Blanc.

WINEMAKER: Karen Steinwachs.

ANNUAL PRODUCTION: 8,500 cases.

OF SPECIAL NOTE: Winery hosts many special events, including Red, White, and Blues concert in June; peach celebration in July; All Buttonwood Farm dinner in August; and Pomegranate Festival and Holiday Open House in December. Fresh peach sales in July and August. Garden picnic area under buttonwood trees.

NEARBY ATTRACTIONS: Mattei's Tavern and other historic buildings in Los Olivos and Ballard; Clairmont Farm Lavender Company; Quicksilver Miniature Horse Ranch; Windhaven Glider Rides; historic Mission Santa Inés.

CAMBRIA ESTATE WINERY

CAMBRIA ESTATE WINERY
5475 Chardonnay Ln.
Santa Maria, CA 93454
805-938-7318
info@cambriawines.com
www.cambriawines.com

OWNER: Barbara Banke.

LOCATION: 12 miles east of
downtown Santa Maria.

APPELLATION: Santa Maria
Valley.

HOURS: 10 A.M.–5 P.M. daily.

TASTINGS: $7 for 7 wines.

TOURS: Monday–Friday
by appointment only. Fee
($10) includes tasting and
informational materials.

THE WINES: Chardonnay,
Pinot Gris, Pinot Noir,
Pinot Noir Vin Gris, Syrah,
Viognier.

SPECIALTIES: Vineyard-
designated Pinot Noirs
and Chardonnays.

WINEMAKER:
Denise Shurtleff.

ANNUAL PRODUCTION:
100,000 cases.

OF SPECIAL NOTE: Gift shop
with cookbooks, clothing,
and small selection of deli
foods. Small patio with
tables adjacent to tasting
room. Picnic area on knoll
overlooking vineyards.
Single-clone estate
Chardonnays and Pinot
Noirs, Rae's Chardonnay,
Vin Gris, Pinot Gris, and
Estrella Clone Syrah available only in tasting room.

NEARBY ATTRACTION:
Colson Canyon Road
Mountain Bike and Hiking
Trail.

In the far northeast corner of Santa Barbara County, the Santa Maria Bench straddles the ancient, gravelly banks of the Sisquoc River. The native Chumash called the area *tepuztli*, or "copper coin." Later, Spanish settlers called it Tepusquet (*tep*-us-kay). The steep slopes of the Tepusquet Mountains rise from the valley north of the bench, creating an unobstructed funnel for the cooling coastal breezes and fog that flow from the ocean seventeen miles to the west. In 1970 and 1971, pioneering Central Coast vitculturalist Louis Lucas and partners George Lucas and Alfred Gagnon planted Tepusquet Vineyard along this remarkable benchland, part of the 1838 Rancho Tepusquet Mexican land grant. The grapes thrived, and winemakers began to covet the fruit grown on the Santa Maria Bench for the rich, expressive character that the *terroir* imparts to cool-climate varieties such as Pinot Noir, Chardonnay, and Syrah.

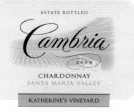

In 1986 Barbara Banke, proprietor of several family-owned California wineries, purchased a portion of the original Tepusquet Vineyard. She established Cambria Estate Winery the next year to produce single-vineyard and small-block Chardonnays and Pinot Noirs, along with small quantities of Syrah and Viognier. Today Cambria Estate Winery occupies fourteen hundred southwest-facing acres and includes a winery, cellar, and tasting room. Banke named two of the four sustainably farmed estate vineyards after her daughters, Katherine and Julia; the other two include Tepusquet, in honor of the historic origins, and Bench Break, on the steepest slope above the estate.

Cambria has identified seventeen distinct soil types and many microclimates on the estate, and recently began replanting vineyard blocks to apply knowledge gained from more than two decades of experimentation. Many blocks are farmed and harvested individually according to their unique soils, microclimate, and elevation. Head winemaker Denise Shurtleff, who joined Cambria in 1999 after sixteen years at Corbett Canyon Vineyards, crafts most of the handpicked estate grapes into nearly thirty different bottlings. Some Pinot Noir grapes are sold to other wineries, including nearby Kenneth Volk Vineyards, Foxen, and Hitching Post Wines.

A half-mile drive through the vineyards leads to Cambria's stone winery building. The tasting room, tucked in a corner on the top floor of the winery, was completely remodeled in 2006. Copper jugs and spittoons sit on a sleek, L-shaped brushed-concrete bar. An exhibit features photos of the barrel-making process. Glass windows enable visitors to observe winery operations in the barrel storage room below. Visitors can relax on the leather sofa before the fireplace and picnic on a nearby knoll with sweeping views of the Santa Maria Bench and Tepusquet Mountains.

CARHARTT VINEYARD

CARHARTT VINEYARD
2990-A Grand Ave.
Los Olivos, CA 93441
805-693-5100
info@carharttvineyard.com
www.carharttvineyard.com

OWNERS: Mike and Brooke
Carhartt.

LOCATION: Just over
.25 mile from Hwy. 154.

APPELLATION: Santa Ynez
Valley.

HOURS: 11 A.M.–5 P.M. daily,
except Tuesdays.

TASTINGS: $10 for 7 wines.

TOURS: None.

THE WINES: Merlot, Rosé,
Sangiovese, Sauvignon
Blanc, Syrah, Zinfandel.

SPECIALTIES: Estate Syrah,
Merlot, Rosé.

WINEMAKERS: Brooke
and Mike Carhartt.

ANNUAL PRODUCTION:
2,000 cases.

OF SPECIAL NOTE: The
smallest tasting room in
the county. Owners pour
wine for guests.

NEARBY ATTRACTIONS:
Wildling Art Museum (art
of the American wilder-
ness); Mattei's Tavern and
other historic buildings
in Los Olivos and Ballard;
Clairmont Farm Lavender
Company; Quicksilver
Miniature Horse Ranch.

At the northern end of Grand Avenue, the main street in Los Olivos, sits an unassuming 1950s wooden cottage covered with climbing roses—the Carhartt Vineyard tasting room. Nearly everything here, indoors and out, reflects a sense of place—of deep connections to the land and people. Wooden tubs with flowers line the walkway and extend from the cottage down the block. On most days, owner Mike Carhartt welcomes visitors into the intimate space and, at the faux stone bar, proudly pours tastes of wines that he has handcrafted with his wife, Brooke. Behind the cottage, Japanese maples and a neighbor's pepper tree shade a cozy patio and garden.

The Carhartt connection to the Santa Ynez Valley took root long ago. A descendant of Hamilton Carhartt, founder of the famed Carhartt Overall Company, Mike grew up on the family's historic Rancho Santa Ynez, a  large cattle and horse ranch. In 1993 he and Brooke acquired fifty acres of the former family estate. Mike had been around farming all of his life and had watched the Santa Ynez Valley develop into a premier wine region, so it made perfect sense for him to devote a portion of the ranch to wine grapes. In 1996 he and Brooke planted ten acres on a six-hundred-foot mesa with optimal conditions for growing Rhône and Bordeaux varietals: maximum sun exposure, warm afternoons, cool evenings, and sandy loam soil.

At first the Carhartts sold most of their fruit to other winemakers. They converted a hay barn into a winery, and Brooke studied enology. In 1998, the first year of fruit production, they vinified two barrels for their own label bearing the Carhartt cattle brand. These early Merlots and Syrahs garnered favorable reviews and awards, so they continued to develop their own program and soon had enough wine to open a tasting room. Their current estate plantings include Merlot, Syrah, Sauvignon Blanc, and Grenache; they also grow Sangiovese at neighboring Eleven Oaks Vineyard and purchase Cabernet Franc, Cabernet Sauvignon, and Zinfandel from other sources.

Although the Carhartts spend much of their time in the tasting room, Brooke still manages all of the winemaking, and Mike spends part of every day in the vineyard. Their son Chase is studying viticulture and enology. The third generation of Carhartts to work the ranchland, he helps out in the summers and, if he chooses, will be well prepared for a major role in the family enterprise.

CARR VINEYARDS & WINERY

CARR VINEYARDS & WINERY
414 N. Salsipuedes St.
Santa Barbara, CA 93103
805-965-7985
info@carrwinery.com
www.carrwinery.com

OWNER: Ryan Carr.

LOCATION: 6 blocks east of
State St. at E. Gutierrez St.

APPELLATIONS: Santa Ynez
Valley, Sta. Rita Hills.

HOURS: 11 A.M.–5 P.M. daily.

TASTINGS: $10 for 5 wines.
Reservations requested for
8 or more guests. $12 tast-
ing fee for groups over 20.

TOURS: None.

THE WINES: Cabernet
Franc, Grenache,
Pinot Gris, Pinot Noir,
Sangiovese, Syrah.

SPECIALTIES: Cabernet
Franc, Pinot Gris,
Pinot Noir.

WINEMAKER:
Ryan Carr.

ANNUAL PRODUCTION:
3,500 cases.

OF SPECIAL NOTE:
Special Friday evening
tastings held in August.
Winemaker dinners and
other events scheduled
year-round.

NEARBY ATTRACTIONS:
East Beach and Cabrillo
Bathhouse (city of Santa
Barbara's main beach);
Santa Barbara Zoo; Santa
Barbara Waterfront Dis-
trict; historic Mission Santa
Barbara; Santa Barbara
Museum of Art.

Carr Winery, in the heart of downtown Santa Barbara, ranks among the most distinctive tasting rooms in the region. The red and white Quonset hut, which resembles a wine cave, originally served as a military barracks at Santa Barbara Airport during World War II. In 2006 winemaker Ryan Carr seized the opportunity to open a new winery and tasting room in the hut, which offered everything he sought: ample space for winemaking operations (forty-five hundred square feet), a downtown location, and easy access via walking, cycling, or public transportation.

Ryan and his wife, Jessica, who serves as director of sales and marketing, immediately began transforming the hut into an efficient winemaking operation and attractive tasting room. They added eco-friendly insulation, tasting bar made by hand from eye-catching works of art such clutching a wineglass and a forty-in college. Outside, a tiny patio and umbrella-shaded tables beck-winery. The door opens to a cool, can view the oak and stainless

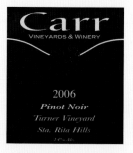

fashioned a striking wraparound wine barrels, and decorated with as a whimsical robot figurine five-pound longboard Ryan built with redwood Adirondack chairs ons visitors to stop and enter the cavernous room, where guests steel wine barrels, play tabletop shuffleboard, and listen to music while tasting Ryan's ultrapremium, limited-production wines. In the fall, visitors can watch Ryan and staff make and bottle wine in the same space.

Before launching his winemaking career, Ryan Carr studied plant science and majored in graphic design at the University of Arizona. After college, Carr headed to Santa Ynez, determined to build a career in winemaking. One of his first jobs was very hands-on—working in the fields for a local vineyard management company. In 1998 he was presented with the opportunity to make wine for Stolpman Vineyards at Central Coast Wine Services. A year later, he produced his first vintage—a total of ten cases—using grapes from a vineyard where he worked. The success of this initial effort inspired him to establish his own vineyard development company and winery.

Today Carr Vineyards supervises more than a hundred acres of vineyards throughout Santa Barbara County, including Paredon (Syrah and Grenache), Morehouse (Syrah), Susich (Syrah), Turner (Pinot Noir, Syrah, and Pinot Gris), and Kessler-Haak (Pinot Noir and Chardonnay). All Carr wines are made from Santa Barbara County grapes grown to Ryan Carr's exact specifications. He now specializes in Pinot Noir, Pinot Gris, and Cabernet Franc. Carr is a big fan of Grenache, but produces it in extremely limited quantities. He spends much of his time outdoors in the vineyards, but often stops by the winery to chat with visitors about his latest vintages.

CONSILIENCE

Brett Escalera grew up watching his grandfathers make wine at home and knew at an early age that he wanted to have a career in the business. He began in 1985 with part-time, seasonal jobs in the cellar with winemaker Bruce McGuire of Santa Barbara Winery. Then he studied enology and viticulture at Cal State Fresno, where he eventually earned a master's degree in agricultural chemistry. Since then, Brett has had stints at various wineries, including Byron, Fess Parker, and Central Coast Wine Services.

While attending school, Brett worked as a Santa Barbara County paramedic and often passed through the Santa Barbara Cottage Hospital emergency room—where he met radiologist Tom Daughters. Through conversations, they discovered a mutual interest in the world of wine. Tom, Brett, and their wives, Jodie Boulet-Daughters and Monica Escalera, toured Napa and Sonoma wine country together. The wine-touring adven-

ture changed their lives forever. Smitten with the idea of starting a winery, Tom and Brett soon made their concept reality. Brett brought extensive viticultural knowledge and winemaking experience to the partnership. Tom approached the enterprise from a different angle as a physician, wine connoisseur, and businessman. Both, however, shared a goal: to create expressive, high-quality, yet reasonably priced wines for people from diverse backgrounds to enjoy in an unpretentious setting. They launched Consilience with a 1997 vintage Syrah, and the label became official in 1999.

The word *consilience* traces its roots to ancient Greek philosophy. Its modern definition, according to Merriam-Webster, is "the linking together of principles from different disciplines especially when forming a comprehensive theory." Everything about the winery, from the three-ring label designs to the tasting room experience—a marriage of the winemakers, tasters, and the wines themselves—reflects this unity of different philosophies and perspectives. Consilience focuses mainly on Rhône varietals, particularly Syrahs, that showcase the diversity of Santa Barbara County vineyards, and has received many accolades for its signature Petite Sirah and highly rated Pinot Noir. Grapes come from approximately fifteen vineyards representing different microclimates.

The wines are most readily available at the casual, six-hundred-square-foot tasting room dressed in warm earth tones in the heart of Los Olivos. Hanging lights cast a soft glow over gift displays, artwork, and the polished concrete bar. On any given day, wine adventurers from all walks of life gather here to sample Brett's creations. On fine-weather days, visitors typically venture outdoors to sit around a picnic table on the quiet, tree-shaded patio and grassy area next door.

CONSILIENCE
2933 Grand Ave.
Los Olivos, CA 93441
805-691-1020
info@consiliencewines.com
www.consiliencewines.com

OWNERS: Tom Daughters, Brett Escalera.

LOCATION: 2 blocks south of Hwy. 154 in downtown Los Olivos.

APPELLATIONS: Santa Maria Valley, Santa Ynez Valley, Sta. Rita Hills.

HOURS: 11 A.M.–5 P.M. daily.

TASTINGS: $10 for 6 wines; $15 for 8 wines (includes complimentary glass).

TOURS: None.

THE WINES: Cabernet Sauvignon, Grenache, Grenache Blanc, Petite Sirah, Pinot Noir, Roussanne, Syrah, Viognier, Zinfandel, Zinfandel Port.

SPECIALTIES: Cabernet Sauvignon, Pinot Noir, Rhône varietals, Zinfandel.

WINEMAKER: Brett Escalera.

ANNUAL PRODUCTION: 8,000 cases.

OF SPECIAL NOTE: Cuvée Mambo, a red varietal blend named after winery dog Mambo, is available only in tasting room. Sister winery Tre Anelli offers Spanish and Italian varietals at tasting room next door.

NEARBY ATTRACTIONS: Wildling Art Museum (art of the American wilderness); Mattei's Tavern and other historic buildings in Los Olivos and Ballard; Clairmont Farm Lavender Company; Quicksilver Miniature Horse Ranch.

COSTA DE ORO WINERY

COSTA DE ORO WINERY
1331 S. Nicholson Ave.
Santa Maria, CA 93454
805-922-1468
info@cdowinery.com
www.cdowinery.com

OWNERS: Burk and
Espinola families.

LOCATION: Just east of U.S.
101 at Stowell Rd. exit.

APPELLATION: Santa Maria
Valley.

HOURS: 11 A.M.–6 P.M. daily.

TASTINGS: $5 for 5 wines;
$10 for 5 reserve wines.

TOURS: None.

THE WINES: Cabernet
Sauvignon, Chardonnay,
Merlot, Pinot Grigio,
Pinot Noir, Sauvignon
Blanc, Syrah.

SPECIALTIES: Estate Pinot
Noir, Chardonnay.

WINEMAKER: Gary Burk.

ANNUAL PRODUCTION:
6,500 cases.

OF SPECIAL NOTE: Farm-
stand with estate-grown
seasonal fruits and veg-
etables on-site. Deli
case with cheeses, meats,
and crackers. Large gift
shop with gourmet foods,
books, and local crafts.
On-site patio and picnic
area. Friday Night Wine
Down with live music
and appetizers from 4:30
to 7:30 P.M. Cabernet Sauvignon, Syrah, Merlot, and
Pinot Grigio available only
in tasting room.

NEARBY ATTRACTIONS: Pacific
Conservatory of the Per-
forming Arts (year-round
theater performances);
Santa Maria Museum
of Flight; Dunes Center
(exhibits on Guadalupe-
Nipomo Dunes Preserve).

Dip a plump, juicy Chandler strawberry in Pinot Noir chocolate sauce and follow it with sips of Costa de Oro wine—then shop for fresh produce from the farm down the road. This scenario typifies the visitor experience at the Costa de Oro tasting room, where locals in the know often line up long before the doors open, not just to taste fine wines, but to nab the best of the fruits and vegetables harvested just hours beforehand.

Costa de Oro Winery is a branch of Gold Coast Farms, founded by Ron Burk and Bob Espinola in 1978 in the heart of the Santa Maria Valley. They planted various crops, including strawberries, broccoli, spinach, cauliflower, and sweet corn. The fruits and vegetables thrived, except on a particular bluff—Fuglar's Point. Burk and Espinola had a hunch that the bluff's well-drained, sandy loam soil, a poor match for vegetables, would make an ideal home for wine grapes. In 1989 the families planted thirty acres, twenty to Pinot Noir and ten to Chardonnay, with vine cuttings from the famed Sierra Madre Vineyard just a few miles away.

The hunch proved correct. Gold Coast Vineyard began producing fruit in the early 1990s. Ron Burk's son Gary, a singer and guitarist, lived in Los Angeles at the time. He supplemented his performance income by selling Gold Coast Vineyard grapes to Au Bon Climat, Foxen, and other local wineries. In 1994 Jim Clendenen, owner/winemaker at Au Bon Climat, and Bob Lindquist, owner/winemaker at Qupé winery at Bien Nacido Vineyards, offered Gary an assistant winemaking position. Gary accepted and simultaneously started producing the first Costa de Oro wines—one barrel each of Pinot Noir and Chardonnay. Gary stayed at Au Bon Climat and Qupé until 2002, when he left to devote his full energies to Costa de Oro. His award-winning wines, praised for their European-style elegance and balance, focus almost exclusively on Pinot Noir and Chardonnay made from estate fruit and other Santa Maria Valley grapes. Gary also sources fruit from other Central Coast vineyards and crafts wines at a shared facility in Santa Maria.

The casual, Tuscan-style Costa de Oro tasting room opened in 2006 at the site of Gold Coast Farm's original strawberry stand, visible from U.S. 101. Tastes are poured at a tasting bar that wraps almost completely around the hosts pouring wines in the center. Windows open up to expansive views across the Santa Maria Valley. Gift items and gourmet foods, including chocolate sauce made with Costa de Oro Pinot Noir, line the tables and display cases. Fruits and vegetables, fresh from Gold Coast Farms, spill from bins in the tasting room and on the outdoor patio—ready to accompany a bottle of Costa de Oro wine at a future meal.

D'ALFONSO-CURRAN WINES

In Santa Barbara County, the names Bruno D'Alfonso and Kris Curran are synonymous with world-class winemaking. D'Alfonso worked from 1983 to 2004 as head winemaker at Sanford Winery, where he crafted internationally acclaimed vintages. Curran met D'Alfonso in the early 1990s, worked at his side during crush, and quickly developed a passion for winemaking. In 2000 she was tapped as head winemaker at Sea Smoke Cellars, where she created some of the nation's most sought-after Pinot Noirs. Eight years later, she was lured away to direct winemaking at Foley Estates Vineyard & Winery. Kris Curran continues her independent winemaking projects, and the husband-and-wife team now collaborates to produce a family of fine wines under the D'Alfonso-Curran label and four other labels. They acquire grapes from topflight area vineyards and make their wines at their winery at Rancho La Viña, in the Santa Rita Hills appellation.

The stylish D'Alfonso-Curran tasting room in downtown Solvang reflects contrasting elements in harmony. Sepia images adorn yellow walls on a warm earth-toned side of the room, and black-and-white photos enhance the opposite blue-themed sector. Silver metal tones are juxtaposed with rustic elements, as in the Italian glass lights and two wood-barrel tasting bars with zinc countertops that complement the leather bar stools and cowhides on the hardwood floor. A flat-screen TV continuously plays a presentation on vineyard harvest, crush, and life within the winery.

The tasting room experience focuses on the wines themselves—and the creative D'Alfonso-Curran duo presents a mind-boggling array of options. Wines bearing the D'Alfonso-Curran label showcase ultrapremium, vineyard-designated Pinot Noirs and Chardonnays exclusively from the Santa Rita Hills. Badge wines feature Pinot Noir and Chardonnay blends from various Santa Rita Hills vineyards. The Santayana line, named for Spanish philosopher/writer George Santayana, highlights Spanish varietals. DiBruno vintages celebrate Bruno D'Alfonso's heritage with red and white Italian varietals. The Curran label concentrates on vineyard-designated Syrahs and a bone-dry Gewürztraminer. D'Alfonso and Curran often hang out in the tasting room along with their four German Shepherds, happy to share their extensive knowledge of winemaking with visitors.

D'Alfonso-Curran

2006
STA RITA HILLS
PINOT NOIR

Rancho La Viña

D'ALFONSO-CURRAN WINES
1557 Mission Dr.
Solvang, CA 93463
805-688-3494
info@d-cwines.com
www.dalfonso-curranwines.com

OWNERS: Kris Curran, Bruno D'Alfonso.

LOCATION: 3 miles east of U.S. 101 on Hwy. 246 (Mission Dr.).

APPELLATIONS: Santa Ynez Valley, Sta. Rita Hills.

HOURS: 11 A.M.–5 P.M. daily, or by appointment.

TASTINGS: $10 for 4 wines; $15 for 6 reserve wines.

TOURS: Winery/vineyard tours with barrel tasting available by appointment, depending on winemaker's availability.

THE WINES: Carignane, Chardonnay, Gewürztraminer, Grenache, Grenache Blanc, Grenache Gris, Merlot, Nebbiolo, Pinot Grigio, Pinot Noir, Sangiovese, Syrah, Tempranillo.

SPECIALTIES: Vineyard-designated Pinot Noirs and Chardonnays, vineyard-designated Syrahs, Spanish varietals.

WINEMAKERS: Kris Curran, Bruno D'Alfonso.

ANNUAL PRODUCTION: 8,000 cases.

OF SPECIAL NOTE: Food-and-wine pairings available in tasting room by appointment.

NEARBY ATTRACTIONS: Quicksilver Miniature Horse Ranch; Elverhøj Museum of History and Art (exhibits on Danish community in Solvang); Windhaven Glider Rides; historic Mission Santa Inés.

DIERBERG & STAR LANE VINEYARDS

DIERBERG & STAR LANE VINEYARDS
1280 Drum Canyon Rd.
Lompoc, CA 93436
866-652-8430
info@dierbergvineyard.com
www.dierbergvineyard.com
www.starlanevineyard.com

OWNERS: Jim and
Mary Dierberg.

LOCATION: 6 miles west of
Buellton via Hwy. 246.

APPELLATIONS: Sta. Rita
Hills, Santa Ynez Valley,
Santa Maria Valley.

HOURS: 11 A.M.–5 P.M. daily.

TASTINGS: $10 for 6 wines.

TOURS: None.

THE WINES: Cabernet Sauvignon, Chardonnay, Merlot,
Pinot Noir, Sauvignon
Blanc, Syrah.

SPECIALTIES: Cabernet
Sauvignon, Pinot Noir.

WINEMAKER:
Nicolas DeLuca.

ANNUAL PRODUCTION:
25,000 cases.

OF SPECIAL NOTE: Picnic
tables on-site. Scenic views
of Santa Rita Hills and
landscaped gardens.

NEARBY ATTRACTIONS:
Historic Mission La
Purísima; Old Town Lompoc Heritage Walk (1-mile
scenic tour with 18 stops);
Jalama Beach County Park
(tidepooling, nature trails,
camping, surfing).

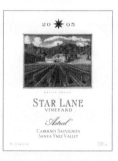

Jim and Mary Dierberg fell in love with Star Lane Ranch at first sight in 1996. Bankers by profession, they have owned one of America's oldest wineries, in their home state of Missouri, since 1974. But they dreamt of crafting ultrapremium Pinot Noir and Cabernet from their own estate fruit in an appellation conducive to growing these varietals. For a decade they searched for possible sites in Bordeaux, Napa, and Paso Robles before discovering Star Lane—an isolated, four-thousand-acre former dude ranch in Happy Canyon, fourteen miles east of Santa Ynez.

The Dierbergs quickly decided that Santa Barbara County, with its desirable east-west orientation and diverse microclimates, held the most promise for their winegrowing ambitions. They bought Star Lane and over the next two years planted 230 acres of Cabernet, Sauvignon Blanc, Syrah, Cabernet Franc, and other varietals ideally suited to the warm, sunny days in the area. In 1996 they also acquired a cooler vineyard site ideal for Pinot Noir and Chardonnay farther north in the Santa Maria Valley, and planted 160 acres to those varietals. In 2005 the Dierbergs added a new vineyard property in the Santa Rita Hills, thirty miles west of Star Lane, also focused mainly on Pinot Noir and Chardonnay.

The three estate vineyards provide all the grapes for the winery's award-winning vintages, bottled and marketed under two separate labels to reflect the distinct growing climates and soil types. Star Lane Vineyard wines showcase Bordeaux varietals from the warmer Happy Canyon—the easternmost and the highest-elevation vineyard in the county. Water from a spring at the 2,800-foot elevation flows down 1,500 feet to Star Lane's new gravity-flow winery, providing hydroelectric power to operate all the equipment and twenty-eight thousand square feet of caves. The spring water—so pure that the previous owner sold it to Air France to bottle for passengers—is also used to wash fruit after harvest. Dierberg Estate Vineyard wines feature Pinot Noir and Chardonnay from the two cooler-climate vineyards closer to the coast, as well as Syrah grown at Star Lane.

Visitors can taste both Star Lane and Dierberg wines at the tasting room located on the Dierberg Estate Vineyard in the Santa Rita Hills. A scenic drive from Buellton toward the ocean leads through peaceful farmland to the green and red building reminiscent of a simple barn on a midwestern farm. At the walnut bar in the contemporary tasting room, each guest samples wines in two separate glasses, one for each label. The absence of a gift shop enables visitors to focus on the wines and discover the sense of place—the *terroir* that defines each of the various vintages, from multiple microclimates in three different appellations.

EPIPHANY CELLARS

It's nearly impossible to miss the large copper letter *E* mounted on a six-foot slab of flagstone that fronts a yellow and white Victorian with a wraparound porch. On sunny days, the letter sparkles with beams of light, beckoning visitors to enter the Epiphany Cellars tasting room. The *E* represents the word *epiphany*, which refers to an instant of sudden insight and revelation. It anchors the Epiphany label and reflects the tone of the tasting room: an inspirational place where visitors can enjoy an intimate wine-tasting experience and leave with new insights on wine.

Epiphany is the brainchild of Eli Parker, son of winery owner and former television celebrity Fess Parker, and a key member of the Fess Parker Winery team since 1988. Eli already had access

to quality grapes and had extensive
more creative outlet for his talents.
track, esoteric wines that wouldn't
traditional portfolio. Specifically, he
Rhône varietals and blends in a flex-
sister Ashley also wanted to develop
terprise of their own. They embarked
released the first vintage in 2000 with
efforts began to pay off quickly,
André Tchelistcheff Winemaker of
International Wine Competition,
United States. Winemaker Blair Fox,
Winery off and on since 1999, be-
in 2005. Fox wasted no time earning
André Tchelistcheff Winemaker of

winemaking expertise but sought a
He wanted to make off-the-beaten
fit with Fess Parker Winery's more
longed to experiment with different
ible, small-lot format. Eli and his
a second-generation winemaking en-
on the Epiphany project in 1999 and
only a thousand cases. Eli's creative
and in 2006 he won the prestigious
the Year Award at the San Francisco
the largest wine competition in the
who had assisted Eli at Fess Parker
came Epiphany's head winemaker
his own accolades: he received the
the Year Award in 2008.

Epiphany's eclectic lineup gives visitors the chance to taste various wines they may never have tried before. Epiphany's Australian-inspired flagship wine, Revelation, pays homage to traditional Rhône blends. Other favorites include Gypsy, a light, delicate blend made predominantly of Grenache and Mourvèdre, and the vineyard-designated Petite Sirah from century-old California clones.

Visitors taste the array of vintages at the brushed-concrete bar in the light-filled tasting room. Copper accents, black walnut floors, local art and photography, and a wine hutch made from part of an old barn reinforce the contemporary-casual feeling and inspire conversation among guests from diverse backgrounds. What starts as a tasting session often leads to epiphanies and new perspectives on the world of wine.

EPIPHANY CELLARS
2963 Grand Ave.
Los Olivos, CA 93441
805-686-2424
866-354-9463
julie@epiphanycellars.com
www.epiphanycellars.com

OWNERS: Parker family.

LOCATION: 1 block south of Hwy. 154.

APPELLATION: Santa Ynez Valley.

HOURS: 11:30 A.M.–5:30 P.M. daily.

TASTINGS: $5 for 6 wines. Additional $5 for souvenir wineglass. Reservations necessary for groups of 8 or more.

TOURS: None.

THE WINES: Dry Riesling, Grenache, Grenache Blanc, Grenache Rosé, Petite Sirah, red Rhône blend, Roussanne, Syrah, Syrah–Cabernet Sauvignon, white Rhône blend.

SPECIALTY: Revelation (Syrah, Grenache, Petite Sirah blend).

WINEMAKER: Blair Fox.

ANNUAL PRODUCTION: 5,000–6,000 cases.

OF SPECIAL NOTE: Many wines available only in tasting room: Roussanne, Inspiration (white Rhône blend), Grenache, Syrah-Cabernet, and several vineyard-designated Syrahs. Picnic tables in front of tasting room. Small gift shop.

NEARBY ATTRACTIONS: Wildling Art Museum (art of the American wilderness); Mattei's Tavern and other historic buildings in Los Olivos and Ballard; Clairmont Farm Lavender Company; Quicksilver Miniature Horse Ranch.

FESS PARKER WINERY & VINEYARDS

FESS PARKER WINERY & VINEYARDS

6200 Foxen Canyon Rd.
Los Olivos, CA 93441
805-688-1545
800-841-1104
tasting@fessparker.com
www.fessparker.com

OWNERS: Fess Parker family.

LOCATION: 1.5 miles east of intersection of Foxen Canyon Rd. and Zaca Station Rd.

APPELLATION: Santa Ynez Valley.

HOURS: 10 A.M.–5 P.M. daily.

TASTINGS: $10 for 6 wines (includes crystal logo glass).

TOURS: None.

THE WINES: Chardonnay, Frontier Red (red Rhône blend), Pinot Noir, Syrah, Viognier, White Riesling.

SPECIALTIES: Rhône and Burgundian varietals.

WINEMAKER: Blair Fox.

ANNUAL PRODUCTION: 65,000 cases.

OF SPECIAL NOTE: Extensive gift shop with wine and home accessories, food and wine books, gourmet foods, and other merchandise. Large, grassy picnic area; bistro tables under veranda. Winery hosts summer evening performances by Shakespeare Santa Barbara theater troupe. Events include Foxen Canyon Wine Trail Autumn Adventure (November). American Tradition Reserve Pinot Noir, Syrah, and Chardonnay available only in tasting room. Winery also operates a hotel and spa.

NEARBY ATTRACTIONS: Wildling Art Museum (art of the American wilderness); Mattei's Tavern and other historic buildings in Los Olivos and Ballard.

Driving north along the pastoral Foxen Canyon Wine Trail feels like traveling back to California's early days. Rolling hills frame vast meadows, deer and wildlife roam free, and pristine landscapes stretch as far as the eye can see. This peaceful environment enticed Fess Parker into buying a 714-acre ranch here back in 1988. The Texas-born actor, who played the television roles of Davy Crockett and Daniel Boone in the 1950s and 1960s, had moved his family to Santa Barbara in the early 1960s and begun construction of a blufftop home. When heavy rains caused it to collapse onto the beach, he revised his plans and headed inland.

There, he discovered the Foxen Canyon property, where he initially planned to run cattle, plant a few grapes to sell to other vintners, and establish a small winery. Parker, an only child, dreamed of starting a family business that he could pass on to future generations. He asked his children to join him, and they planted a five-acre experimental White Riesling vineyard in 1989. Eli, his son, started as assistant winemaker and spent three years under the tutelage of acclaimed enologist Jed Steele before taking the helm. Eli then planted more vines and started a four-year project to build a cutting-edge winery and tasting room.

Eli Parker is now president of Fess Parker Winery & Vineyards. His sister Ashley is vice-president, and her husband, Tim Snider, is CEO. The vineyards include the 120-acre Rodney's Vineyard, named after Fess Parker's late son-in-law, at the 400-acre Foxen Canyon Road estate, and a 230-acre vineyard at Camp 4 in the heart of Santa Ynez Valley, planted in 1998. They also source grapes from vineyards in the cooler Santa Rita Hills and Santa Maria Valley appellations. Blair Fox assumed the role of head winemaker in 2005. In recent years, the winery has sharpened its focus to produce more small-lot, vineyard-designated wines made from high-quality Rhône and Burgundian varietals, which have won awards in national wine competitions.

Completed in 1994, the new winery and tasting room are loosely designed after an Australian sheep station, with a grand stone fireplace, stone floors, and a wraparound veranda with picnic tables. The spacious complex is set amid an acre of meticulously landscaped grounds that border the vineyard. The amphitheater-style lawn, rimmed by mature oaks, provides a serene setting for picnics, summer evening performances by Shakespeare Santa Barbara, and other events. Indoors, visitors taste the latest vintages at a worn knotty pine bar, surrounded by photos of Fess Parker as Davy Crockett and Daniel Boone and other memorabilia related to the actor's television roles.

FOLEY ESTATES VINEYARD & WINERY

Along Highway 246 between Lompoc and Buellton, a stunning scene leaps into view from the roadside: a series of fifty-nine vineyard blocks blanketing steep, south-facing hillsides and the gently sloping valley below. The setting is Rancho Santa Rosa, home of Foley Estates Vineyard & Winery and part of the original fifteen-thousand-acre parcel granted by the Mexican government to former Presidio officer Francisco Cota's ten children in 1845.

Vintner Bill Foley, owner of Lincourt Vineyards in the Santa Ynez Valley since 1994, had successfully produced varietals suited for the region's warm climate. However, he hoped to establish a separate vineyard estate to focus on Pinot Noir, Chardonnay, Syrah, and other varietals that would thrive in the limestone  soils and cooling maritime effects of the Santa Rita Hills appellation. In 1998, with topographical maps and data from extensive soil and climate research in hand, he scoured the region and discovered an ideal site—the 460-acre Rancho Santa Rosa, a thoroughbred horse ranch with various microclimates and elevations from five hundred to a thousand feet above sea level. He then launched an ambitious microfarming project patterned after practices common in Burgundy's Côtes d'Or. He divided 230 acres of planted vines into fifty-nine small blocks (average size less than 4 acres), each farmed, harvested, and vinified separately according to specifications unique to the particular soils, microclimate, and elevation. Foley also refurbished the former stables to house a 12,000-square-foot, state-of-the-art winery, and completed an adjacent 3,500-square-foot tasting room and event center in 2005.

The Foley Estates Burgundian-influenced wines, highly regarded by wine critics and sommeliers, are known for their diversity and rich character. Estate vineyard blocks now include Pinot Noir, Syrah, Cinsault, Pinot Gris, Grenache, Grüner Veilteiner, Gewürztraminer, and Pinot Grigio. Winemaker Kris Curran helped set up nearby Sea Smoke Cellars in 2000 and headed its winemaking team for eight years, achieving international recognition for crafting exceptional Pinot Noir from Sea Smoke's Santa Rita Hills estate fruit. In 2008 Foley lured Curran away from Sea Smoke Cellars to become director of winemaking at Foley Estates.

The tasting room, in the spacious hospitality center, reflects the ranch's historic Spanish/Mexican roots in contemporary mission style, with light wood floors, a curved cherrywood tasting bar, and shelves displaying myriad gifts for purchase. Guests sink into leather armchairs near a stone fireplace and enjoy the magnificent views of the surrounding oak-studded hills and multifaceted vineyard that defines the modern Rancho Santa Rosa.

FOLEY ESTATES VINEYARD & WINERY
6121 E. Hwy. 246
Lompoc, CA 93436
805-737-6222
info@foleywinegroup.com
www.foleywinegroup.com

OWNER: William Foley II.

LOCATION: 10 miles west of Buellton on Hwy. 246.

APPELLATION: Sta. Rita Hills.

HOURS: 10 A.M.–5 P.M. daily.

TASTINGS: $10 for 5 wines.

TOURS: None.

THE WINES: Chardonnay, Pinot Gris, Pinot Noir, Rosé (Syrah, Cinsault, Grenache blend), Syrah.

SPECIALTIES: Estate-grown Pinot Noir and Chardonnay from specific vineyard blocks.

WINEMAKER: Kris Curran.

ANNUAL PRODUCTION: 20,000 cases.

OF SPECIAL NOTE: Picnic areas on-site, some under patio awning. Well-stocked gift shop with clothing, books, gourmet food items, and wine-themed crafts. Certain block-designated Chardonnay and Pinot Noir vintages available only in tasting room.

NEARBY ATTRACTIONS: Historic Mission La Purísima; Old Town Lompoc Heritage Walk (1-mile scenic tour with 18 stops); Jalama Beach County Park (tidepooling, nature trails, camping, surfing).

FOXEN

FOXEN
7200 Foxen Canyon Rd.
Santa Maria, CA 93454
805-937-4251
info@foxenvineyard.com
www.foxenvineyard.com

OWNERS: Richard Doré,
Bill Wathen.

LOCATION: 16 miles north
of Hwy. 154.

APPELLATIONS: Santa Maria
Valley, Santa Ynez Valley,
Sta. Rita Hills.

HOURS: 11 A.M.–4 P.M. daily.

TASTINGS: $12. Reservations
required for groups of
8 or more.

TOURS: None.

THE WINES: Cabernet
Franc, Cabernet Sauvi-
gnon, Chardonnay, Chenin
Blanc, Cuvée Jeanne-
Marie (Grenache, Syrah,
Mourvèdre blend), Merlot,
Pinot Noir, Sangiovese,
Sauvignon Blanc, Syrah.

SPECIALTIES: Chardonnay,
small-lot, vineyard-
designated Pinot Noir,
Syrah.

WINEMAKER: Bill Wathen.

ANNUAL PRODUCTION:
10,000 cases.

OF SPECIAL NOTE: New tasting room is scheduled for
completion by summer/
fall 2009. Open houses
in April and October.
Picnic tables on-site. Late
Harvest Old-Vine Chenin
Blanc, some bottlings of
Pinot Noir, and Tinaquaic
Vineyard Cabernet Franc
and Syrah available only in
tasting room.

NEARBY ATTRACTION:
Historic 1875 San Ramon
Chapel (Benjamin Foxen
Memorial Chapel).

At the northern reaches of the Foxen Canyon Wine Trail, the scenic country road leads to a vast and isolated region that the native Chumash called Tinaquaic, "little creek" or "gathering place." Benjamin William Foxen, an English sea captain, was the earliest pioneer in the area. The Mexican governor granted Foxen the 8,874-acre Rancho Tinaquaic on May 16, 1837, where his family later built a two-story English country home, barns, a harness shop, corrals, and other structures near the banks of spring-fed Tinaquaic Creek. He also created a distinctive brand for his horses and cattle—an anchor symbolizing his connection with the sea.

Nearly two thousand acres of the original Rancho Tinaquaic still belong to the Foxen family. Foxen's great-great-grandson, maker/business partner Bill wines just steps from his family's a redwood shack with a cor- blacksmith shop where horse- buildings, including a white barn storage shed with tin roof, date

Dick Doré, along with wine- Wathen, produces sought-after old home. The tasting room, rugated tin roof, is the former shoes were forged. All the nearby with weathervane and a brown to the 1880s or earlier.

Bill Wathen and Dick Doré, who call themselves the Foxen Boys, founded their winery in 1985 on a shoestring, using the historic Foxen anchor brand on the label. Wathen, an up-and-coming viticulturalist, had worked with famed California winemaking pioneer Dick Graff at Chalone. While Doré marketed the business, Wathen crafted the wines, using grapes from the Tinaquaic estate and other vineyard blocks they farmed at nearby Bien Nacido Block 8, Ernesto Wickenden, and Williamson-Doré. Starting with Chenin Blanc, Chardonnay, Pinot Noir, and Cabernet Sauvignon, they gradually expanded and refined their production. A decade ago, they added Rhône varietals. Now, the Foxen Boys devote half of their production to their intense, yet balanced Pinot Noirs, including a highly sought-after version made from Santa Rita Hills Sea Smoke Vineyard grapes. Foxen is the only winery other than Sea Smoke with access to these grapes.

Wathen and Doré use sustainable methods to dry-farm the ten-acre estate vineyard, planted with Chardonnay, Syrah, and Cabernet Franc. Just down the road, they recently planted a five-acre organic vineyard with Cabernet Franc and Syrah, and began constructing a solar-powered winery and tasting room. The new facility will focus on Pinot Noir, Chardonnay, and Syrah. Visitors to the winery's original site, soon to be known as Foxen 7200, beloved for its quirky and irreverent atmosphere, will continue to enjoy tastes of Foxen's Bordeaux and California-Italian wines, surrounded by historic photos, antique furnishings, and other reminders of Benjamin Foxen's pioneering legacy.

GAINEY VINEYARD

The vast Gainey Ranch epitomizes the Santa Ynez Valley lifestyle, where farming, ranching, and equestrian pursuits go in tandem. In 1962 hardy Minnesotans Dan C. Gainey and his son Dan J. purchased eighteen hundred acres stretching along the banks of the Santa Ynez River and into the foothills. They continued to run an existing cattle business and launched a large-scale farming operation. In the early 1980s, Dan J. and his son Dan H. foresaw the potential to produce quality grapes, and planted a fifty-acre vineyard in 1983. In 1984 they constructed a Spanish-style winery, designing it with the visitor in mind, at a time when the valley had few tasting rooms.

Today thousands of visitors come annually, not just to taste Gainey wines, but to witness life on a diverse working ranch. Cattle roam nearly a thousand acres on the oak-studded slopes of the Santa Ynez Mountains. More  than six hundred acres are devoted to a range of crops: alfalfa and forage grasses, organic vegetables (such as peppers, squash, corn, broccoli, pumpkin, onions) and fruits (occasionally melons), and flowers for seed. An Arabian horse breeding and training facility occupies about a hun- dred acres of the estate. Grapes are grown on about a hundred acres at the Home Ranch in Santa Ynez, and more than a hundred acres at Evans Ranch (named for Dan H.'s great-grandfather) and another holding in the Santa Rita Hills—all distinct microclimates that provide the chance to grow many different varietals.

The Home Ranch vineyards are planted in Bordeaux varietals that tend to thrive in warmer conditions: Sauvignon Blanc, Merlot, Cabernet Sauvignon, and Cabernet Franc. The Santa Rita Hills vineyards, where temperatures average fifteen to twenty degrees cooler than the valley, focus on Chardonnay, Pinot Noir, and Syrah. Winemaker Kirby Anderson, who has crafted Gainey wines for more than a decade, now aims to transform the Santa Rita Hills grapes into creative new vintages. To the east, in Santa Ynez Valley, Jon Engelskirger oversees winemaking sourced from the estate's Bordeaux varietals. Gainey Vineyard's Limited Selection wines, made from specific vineyard sections groomed to produce low yields and intense flavors, receive consistent critical praise. These typically feature Sauvignon Blanc, Chardonnay, Pinot Noir, Syrah, and several Bordeaux.

A visit to Gainey Vineyard should always be timed to include one of the popular, comprehensive tours of the gravity-flow winery. The hospitality center resembles a Spanish-style hacienda, with wooden benches and doors, wrought-iron embellishments, Spanish tile floors, and high-beamed ceilings. Outdoors, pepper trees line the long entrance drive that leads to an expansive lawn with tables and an arbor-shaded veranda—excellent spots for a picnic and observing ranch life firsthand.

GAINEY VINEYARD
3950 E. Hwy. 246
Santa Ynez, CA 93460
805-688-0558
info@gaineyvineyard.com
www.gaineyvineyard.com

OWNER: Dan H. Gainey.

LOCATION: Off Hwy. 246, .5 mile west of Hwy. 154.

APPELLATIONS: Santa Ynez Valley, Sta. Rita Hills.

HOURS: 10 A.M.–5 P.M. daily.

TASTINGS: $10 for 7–9 wines.

TOURS: 11 A.M., 1 P.M., 2 P.M., and 3 P.M. daily. Appointment necessary for groups of 8 or more.

THE WINES: Cabernet Sauvignon, Chardonnay, Merlot, Pinot Noir, Riesling, Sauvignon Blanc, Syrah.

SPECIALTIES: Limited-production wines from selected vineyards.

WINEMAKERS: Kirby Anderson (Burgundian varietals); Jon Engelskirger (Bordeaux varietals).

ANNUAL PRODUCTION: 30,000 cases.

OF SPECIAL NOTE: Open house during Santa Barbara County Vintner's Festival (weekends in April and October). Annual Crush Party (September). Deli items sold on-site. Limited Selection wines available only in tasting room.

NEARBY ATTRACTIONS: Windhaven Glider Rides; historic Mission Santa Inés; Santa Ynez Valley Historical Society Museum (early California exhibits, carriage house, gift shop); Cachuma Lake (county park with boating, fishing, nature cruises).

HITCHING POST WINES

HITCHING POST WINES
The Hitching Post II
406 E. Hwy. 246
Buellton, CA 93427
805-688-0676
info@hpwines.com
www.hpwines.com

OWNER: Frank Ostini.

LOCATION: 1.5 miles east of U.S. 101.

APPELLATIONS: Santa Maria Valley, Santa Ynez Valley, Sta. Rita Hills.

HOURS: 4–6 P.M. Monday–Friday; 3–5 P.M. Saturday and Sunday (for wine tasting).

TASTINGS: $7 for 6 wines.

TOURS: None.

THE WINES: Cabernet Franc, Merlot, Pinot Noir, Rosé, Syrah.

SPECIALTY: Highliner Pinot Noir.

WINEMAKERS: Gray Hartley, Frank Ostini.

ANNUAL PRODUCTION: 11,000 cases.

OF SPECIAL NOTE: Tastings are held in one of the most popular restaurants in the Santa Ynez Valley. Wines are made by chef-owner to complement menu.

NEARBY ATTRACTIONS: Ostrich Land (33-acre ostrich farm); Elverhøj Museum of History and Art (exhibits on Danish community in Solvang); Windhaven Glider Rides; historic Mission Santa Inés.

It's one thing to pair wines with food. But how many chefs crush, barrel, and bottle the wine served with the food they prepare? Chef-winemaker Frank Ostini set out to accomplish just that in 1979. His parents had operated the popular Hitching Post steak house in Casmalia, near Santa Maria, since 1952. They specialized in Santa Maria–style barbecue—grilling steaks and chops over an open fire of red oak. After Ostini returned from college in 1976, he worked in the Hitching Post kitchen. As a lark, he decided to create his own wines to complement the restaurant's meals. He asked a friend, Gray Hartley, to join him in the backyard project. Hartley agreed, and the duo made a Mer-

lot in an old whiskey barrel. The next year, they produced a Cabernet, followed in 1981 by a Pinot Noir. Pleased with the results of their amateur Pinot Noir, a varietal that had not yet emerged as a regional star, Ostini and Hartley went commercial in 1984 and soon gained critical acclaim for smooth vintages that matched extremely well with food.

In 1991 Hartley Ostini Wines became the official brand of the Hitching Post restaurants. Because Hartley fished commercially in Alaska for more than twenty years, his seafaring days have influenced some of the winery's signature labels: the flagship Highliner Pinot Noir uses a term that refers to the best fisherman in the fleet. As a further reflection of the name, Hartley and Ostini source grapes from prestigious vineyards throughout Santa Barbara County, including Julia's Vineyard, Fiddlestix, Bien Nacido, and Sierra Madre.

Ostini opened the Hitching Post II restaurant in Buellton in 1986. He retained the Santa Maria–style barbecue, but added eclectic local ingredients such as quail and ostrich to the menu. Flights of Hitching Post wines are available for tasting in the wood-paneled lounge area. Bartenders pour the wine samples, and many visitors also order from the appetizer menu. The movie *Sideways* was filmed extensively at the restaurant in 2003, and photos of Ostini and the cast line the walls.

In 2008 Hartley and Ostini moved their winemaking operations from Santa Maria to Terravant Wine Company, a custom winemaking facility in Buellton. Although tastings of Hitching Post wines are offered at Terravant's new visitor center, wine aficionados continue to flock to the ever-popular Hitching Post II, where the chef-winemaker blends his culinary and vinous creations.

JAFFURS WINE CELLARS

Driving north on Milpas Street from U.S. 101 and Santa Barbara's beachfront area leads to the town's vibrant Lower Eastside neighborhood, home of dozens of ethnic restaurants, eclectic shops, industrial zones, and residents representing a melting pot of cultures. Jaffurs Wine Cellars sits in an unlikely but convenient spot for a winery and tasting room, in the heart of this lively district. Those who find Jaffurs reap great rewards: the chance to taste some of the region's finest wines in the same space where they are crushed, pressed, cellared, and bottled.

Craig Jaffurs spent nearly two decades as a cost analyst in the aerospace industry. In the late 1980s, bored with his career and fascinated by Rhône varietals, he began hanging out with winery folk, including backpacking buddy Bruce McGuire, wine-maker at Santa Barbara Winery. McGuire and other friends prodded Jaffurs to get involved in the field, so he volunteered as a cellar rat for McGuire for five harvests. He planted Syrah vines in his backyard, took classes at UC Davis, and experimented with several vintages of Syrah and Chardonnay in his garage before he and his wife, award-winning children's book author Lee Wardlaw, founded their own winery in the early 1990s, using

co-op production facilities in Santa Maria. Their first professional wine, the 1994 Santa Barbara County Syrah, received rave reviews in *Wine Spectator* and *The Wine Advocate*. Many Jaffurs Wine Cellars vintages have continued to garner widespread accolades. The winery doesn't own vineyards, but purchases premium wine grapes from Santa Barbara County vineyards that follow sustainable and/or biodynamic farming practices, including Thompson, Bien Nacido, Larner, Verna's, and Ampelos.

By 1998 Jaffurs had abandoned his aerospace job to run the winery full-time. In 2001 the couple constructed a 3,500-square-foot, Spanish-style winery on a small Milpas District lot. Longtime friend and garage winery helper Dave Yates came on board as general manager in 2003. Matt Brady, a UC Santa Barbara graduate and budding winemaker, joined the team in 2005. All three fill interchangeable hands-on roles, and on any given day visitors are likely to see at least one of them driving forklifts, answering questions, and, during harvest, directing the crush and barreling operations.

Visitors taste wine at various cloth-covered folding tables set up on the concrete floor, next to the destemmer, press, barrels, and tanks. A display of vintage surfboards (part of Craig Jaffurs's collection) and splashes of bright paint liven up the soaring, two-story walls. Every day here offers new perspectives for visitors—tables move around as winery tasks vary—in an environment that perfectly suits Jaffurs's surfer/bohemian spirit and creative winemaking style.

JAFFURS WINE CELLARS
819 E. Montecito St.
Santa Barbara, CA 93103
805-962-7003
info@jaffurswine.com
www.jaffurswine.com

OWNERS: Craig Jaffurs, Lee Wardlaw Jaffurs.

LOCATION: 4 blocks north of Milpas St. exit on U.S. 101.

APPELLATIONS: Santa Maria Valley, Santa Ynez Valley, Sta. Rita Hills.

HOURS: 11 A.M.–5 P.M. Friday–Sunday.

TASTINGS: $10 for 5 wines. Reservations required for groups of 6 or more.

TOURS: Upon request.

THE WINES: Grenache, Mourvèdre, Petite Sirah, Roussanne, Syrah, Viognier.

SPECIALTY: Vineyard-designated Syrah.

WINEMAKER: Craig Jaffurs.

ANNUAL PRODUCTION: 4,000 cases.

OF SPECIAL NOTE: Upslope Syrah (an ultrapremium cuvée) and Whole-Cluster Grenache available only in tasting room. Visitors can watch crush in the driveway during harvest season, and bottling three times a year.

NEARBY ATTRACTIONS: East Beach and Cabrillo Bathhouse (city of Santa Barbara's main beach); Santa Barbara Zoo; Santa Barbara Waterfront District; historic Mission Santa Barbara; Santa Barbara Museum of Art.

KENNETH VOLK VINEYARDS

KENNETH VOLK VINEYARDS
5230 Tepusquet Rd.
Santa Maria, CA 93454
805-938-7896
info@volkwines.com
www.volkwines.com

OWNER: Ken Volk.

LOCATION: 12 miles southeast of downtown Santa Maria.

APPELLATION: Santa Maria Valley.

HOURS: 10:30 A.M.–4:30 P.M. daily.

TASTINGS: $5 for 6 wines. Reservations required for groups of 10 or more ($10 fee).

TOURS: None.

THE WINES: Cabernet Franc, Cabernet Pfeffer, Cabernet Sauvignon, Chardonnay, Claret, Malvasia Bianca, Merlot, Mourvèdre, Negrette, Orange Muscat, Pinot Grigio, Pinot Noir, Syrah, Tempranillo, Verdelho, Zinfandel.

SPECIALTIES: Chardonnay, Pinot Noir, heirloom varietals.

WINEMAKER: Ken Volk.

ANNUAL PRODUCTION: 14,000 cases.

OF SPECIAL NOTE: On-site picnic areas in gardens and shaded deck above creek. Many wines, especially those made from lesser-known varietals, available only in tasting room.

NEARBY ATTRACTION: Colson Canyon Road Mountain Bike and Hiking Trail.

Few people know as much about growing finicky grapes and translating them into first-rate wines as veteran vintner and avid horticulturalist Ken Volk, who has crafted Central Coast wines for nearly three decades. Volk majored in fruit science at Cal Poly San Luis Obispo in the late 1970s and made his first wine in a trash can, stirring it with a baseball bat. In 1981 he and family members established Wild Horse Winery in Templeton, near Paso Robles, and opened one of the earliest wineries and tasting rooms in the region. Wild Horse wines, particularly Pinot Noir, earned a nationwide reputation for excellence, and the business grew into a 150,000-case-per-year enterprise. In 2003 Volk, who yearned to return to a more flexible, small-scale winemaking environment, sold Wild Horse and began the search for a new winery site.

In 2004 Volk purchased a twelve-acre parcel in narrow Tepusquet Canyon, in the far eastern sector of the mineral-rich Santa Maria Bench growing region. The property, perched on a scenic bluff sixty feet above spring-fed Tepusquet Creek, origi- nally belonged to pioneer-ing winemaker Ken Brown, founder of Byron Winery. Brown planted a four-acre Chardonnay vineyard and constructed a small, knotty pine winery building there in 1981. Volk spent much of the next year gutting and outfitting the winery interior to create an efficient, technologically advanced facility appropriate for the production of luxury-class wines. One notable innovation includes an OXO barrel racking system, which helps preserve the delicate aromatics of white wines.

In 2006 Kenneth Volk Vineyards released its first wines, praised as complex with rich character. The winery seeks out exceptional grapes throughout the Central Coast and purchases most fruit from growers Volk has cooperated with for many years. The winery focuses primarily on Chardonnay and Pinot Noir from Santa Maria Valley vineyards, including Sierra Madre, Bien Nacido, Solomon Hills, Garey Ranch, and Nielson. Most Cabernet and Merlot grapes come from western Paso Robles. The diverse lineup of nearly thirty wines also reflects Ken Volk's interest in rare, often underappreciated varietals and heirloom wines such as Negrette, Malvasia Bianca, and Cabernet Pfeffer.

Visitors park near a lawn and lovely gardens with a hummingbird sanctuary that also attracts moths, butterflies, and other beneficial insects. A raised-bed organic vegetable garden occupies a corner of the gardens—amateur plant breeder Ken Volk's hobby. Tastes are poured in a small, rustic room with an antique grape press in a corner. Visitors can sit at the outdoor deck while sampling the most recent releases and gaze over the pristine natural canyon setting just above Tepusquet Creek.

PALMINA

In Italy, wine is an extension of the plate and an integral part of daily life. Friends and family gather around a communal table to share lively conversation, local foods, and wines that complement each part of the meal. Palmina owners Steve and Chrystal Clifton celebrate this lifestyle at their winery and intimate *enoteca*, or wine cellar, designed to make visitors feel as if they're enjoying antipasto and *aperitivo* at the village home of Tuscan friends.

Steve, a former musician and nightclub entrepreneur, began his winemaking career in the tasting room at Rancho Sisquoc. He worked his way into the cellar and eventually became assistant winemaker under veteran Central Coast winemaker Stephan Bedford. He then moved on to other positions at Beckmen, Brander, and Domaine Santa Barbara wineries. In 1995 Steve partnered with Greg Brewer to form Brewer-Clifton, devoted to the Burgundian varietals. That same year, Steve founded Palmina to pursue his passion for northern Italian varietal wines. The success of Brewer-Clifton wines encouraged his efforts with both wineries. Chrystal, who had studied at the University of Bologna, joined the Palmina team in 2000. She and Steve were married in Friuli, Italy, in the spring of 2004.

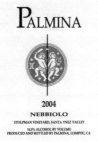

Today Palmina produces seventeen wines from Santa Barbara County vineyards, including Stolpman, Honea, and Larner, and welcomes visitors to taste Steve's translations of Italian varietals into vintages with distinct expressions of the regional *terroir*. Finding the *enoteca* can be tricky. It's at the end of a cul-de-sac, tucked amid warehouses and mostly nondescript business facades in what locals call the Lompoc Wine Ghetto, an industrial zone at the edge of town. Once visitors step through Palmina's entrance, however, they are swept into a different world altogether. The host immediately invites guests to sit on benches at a single family-style wooden table with authentic Italian copper spittoons, or on stools at a narrow bar lining a wall. The table is laden with bread sticks, dipping oils made from local olives or walnuts, homemade salami, and grana cheese. The host serves flights of wines while guests share thoughts of the wines and the world at large.

Every detail in the room reflects pride in both Italian and local culture. A colorful Venetian mask, maps, and photos of the Cliftons' wedding and Old Italy adorn the walls. Italian boxes serve as display shelves, holding wines, books, and gifts for sale. Benches, candleholders, and artworks—all made from barrel staves by a local carpenter—add to the rustic village ambience. One shelf has mason jars with vineyard soil samples, which remind guests of the beginnings of the winemaking cycle and the interconnections of family, community, and earth's bounty.

PALMINA
1520 E. Chestnut Ct.
Lompoc, CA 93436
805-735-2030
info@palminawines.com
www.palminawines.com

OWNERS: Steve and Chrystal Clifton.

LOCATION: .3 mile from Hwy. 246 via 7th Ave.

APPELLATIONS: Sta. Rita Hills, Santa Ynez Valley, Santa Maria Valley.

HOURS: 11 A.M.–4 P.M. Thursday–Sunday; by appointment Monday–Wednesday.

TASTINGS: $10 for 5 wines; $15 for 3 reserve wines. Reservations requested for 9 or more guests. $12 tasting fee for groups over 20.

TOURS: None.

THE WINES: Arneis, Barbera, Dolcetto, Malvasia Bianca, Nebbiolo, Pinot Grigio, Rosato, Sangiovese, Tocai Friulano, Traminer.

SPECIALTY: Vineyard-designated Nebbiolo.

WINEMAKER: Steve Clifton.

ANNUAL PRODUCTION: 10,000 cases.

OF SPECIAL NOTE: Antipasti served with wine tasting. Library tastings held during April Vintner's Festival and October Celebration of Harvest weekends. Winery cooks and hosts a winemaker dinner in August. Black Stripe label and small-lot bottlings available only in tasting room.

NEARBY ATTRACTIONS: Historic Mission La Purísima; Old Town Lompoc Heritage Walk (1-mile scenic tour with 18 stops); Jalama Beach County Park (tidepooling, nature trails, camping, surfing).

STOLPMAN VINEYARDS & WINERY

STOLPMAN VINEYARDS & WINERY
2434 Alamo Pintado Ave.
Los Olivos, CA 93441
805-688-0400
info@stolpmanvineyards.com
www.stolpmanvineyards.com

OWNERS: Tom and Marilyn Stolpman.

LOCATION: .25 mile south of Hwy. 154.

APPELLATION: Santa Ynez Valley.

HOURS: 11 A.M.–5 P.M. Saturday–Thursday; 11 A.M.–6 P.M. Friday.

TASTINGS: $12 for 5 wines.

TOURS: Vineyard tours by appointment. No winery tours.

THE WINES: Angeli, La Croce (Sangiovese, Syrah blend), La Cuadrilla (from a block of fruit chosen annually by vineyard crew), L'Avion (90 percent Roussanne), Sangiovese, Sauvignon Blanc, Syrah, Viognier.

SPECIALTY: Syrah.

WINEMAKER: Sashi Moorman.

ANNUAL PRODUCTION: 7,000 cases.

OF SPECIAL NOTE: Estate olive oil available for purchase (blend of Frantoio, Pendolino, Maurino, and Leccino varieties). Winery holds Dinner in the Vineyard annually in August.

NEARBY ATTRACTIONS: Wildling Art Museum (art of the American wilderness); Mattei's Tavern and other historic buildings in Los Olivos and Ballard; Clairmont Farm Lavender Company; Quicksilver Miniature Horse Ranch.

When Los Angeles–area attorneys Tom and Marilyn Stolpman scoured Santa Barbara County looking for a vineyard site in the late 1980s, they knew exactly what they wanted. They collected wines and had attended wine country events, where they met second-career vintners who weren't afraid of getting their hands dirty. These mavericks inspired the Stolpmans to start a vineyard of their own. They searched throughout the Central Coast for a site with specific requirements: limestone soil, a cool climate with a narrow temperature range, and multiple microclimates for growing various concentrated, intense grapes at the same estate. In 1989 they met and teamed up with vineyard consultant Jeff Newton in Santa Ynez, who recommended a beautiful undeveloped 220-acre estate in Ballard Canyon with great potential for producing flavorful, mineral-rich wines.

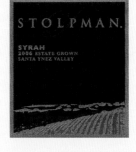

The site choice proved wise. The Stolpmans planted their first grapes in 1992, intending to sell all of them to other vintners. Over the next few years, several wineries produced critically acclaimed wines from Stolpman Vineyards fruit. The Stolpmans decided to retain some of the harvest for their own label and in 1997 bottled their first wines: eight hundred cases of Merlot, Cabernet Franc, and Sangiovese. A year later, the winery released its first Syrah. Since then, Stolpman wines have earned numerous accolades for their elegant, austere character. The vineyards now include 150 acres of grapes, coveted by wineries throughout the Central Coast. The Stolpmans retain 60 percent of the harvest for estate wines; eventually they will retain up to 90 percent of the harvest. The Stolpmans also planted five acres of olives, which are pressed into limited quantities of extra-virgin oil.

Winemaker Sashi Moorman came to Stolpman in 2001 after five years of working with famed winemaker Adam Tolmach at Ojai Vineyard. Moorman focuses on the winery's flagship Syrahs while experimenting with fruit from new, high-density plantings, including Syrah, Sangiovese, Grenache, and Petite Sirah. His Syrahs include Hilltops, from high-elevation blocks, and Gli Angeli, from a single block that produces the most concentrated Syrah grapes on the ranch.

Visitors can sample the latest releases at the tasting room in Los Olivos. This new tasting room, which replaces the previous facility in Solvang, is in a red cottage built in 1923. The interior, transformed to give it a contemporary Tuscan style, has bamboo floors and brightly colored walls. The centerpiece is an unusual S-shaped, brushed-concrete bar. The building also includes a library room for private tastings. Guests can relax outdoors on the covered deck as they savor the results of the Stolpmans' quest for an ideal spot to grow their vines.

SUMMERLAND WINERY

Just before U.S. 101 arrives in Santa Barbara from the south, it passes through Summerland, a serene beach town and art colony. Much of the quaint village stretches along tall bluffs between steep hillsides and the shore, making for stellar views of the Pacific Ocean and Channel Islands. Spas, boutiques, and restaurants line the few short streets of the business district, attracting well-heeled residents from neighboring Montecito.

Summerland Winery Boutique, the winery's tasting room, occupies a two-story clapboard building on the main thoroughfare. Inside, visitors taste Summerland wines in a room decorated with numerous ribbons and medals from wine competitions, plus furnishings and embroidered pillows, rugs, and other gifts imported from Turkey. The Turkish elements reflect owner Nebil "Bilo" Zarif's

heritage. Raised in Turkey and educated in France and the United States, Zarif launched and sold several energy companies before purchasing a three-hundred-acre property and planting a vineyard in the Cuyama Valley, east of Santa Maria, in the early 1990s and later forming a partnership to acquire Laetitia Winery in San Luis Obispo County. He left the partnership in 2001 and a year later established Summerland Winery. Zarif, an avid polo player, selected the town's name for his wines to reflect his fond memories of playing at the nearby Santa Barbara Polo Club. He hired Belgian-born winemaker Etienne Terlinden to craft Summerland wines. Consulting enologist Michelle Pignarre Le Danois, a Bordeaux resident with nearly forty years of winemaking experience, comes to the winery from France every July to lend her blending expertise.

Summerland wines leapt onto the international wine map almost immediately. Robert Parker lauded the 2002 Chardonnay and Pinot Noir made from Bien Nacido Vineyard fruit. Today Summerland produces more than thirty stylish bottlings. Its Single Vineyard Collection showcases vineyard-designated Pinot Noir from three appellations: Santa Rita Hills (Rancho Santa Rosa and Fiddlestix vineyards), Santa Maria Valley (Bien Nacido and Solomon Hills vineyards), and Edna Valley (Odyssey-Thurleston and Wolff vineyards). The blended, moderately priced wines in the Central Coast Collection include Rhône varietals from select vineyards throughout the region.

Summerland Winery Boutique opened its doors in 2004. Visitors taste the diverse array of wines at an intricately carved wooden tasting bar with handpainted Turkish spittoons and are offered samples of cheeses, oils, and nuts. On fine-weather days, visitors often sip wine on the porch, overlooking the tranquil seaside town that inspired the winery name.

SUMMERLAND WINERY
2330 Lillie Ave.
Summerland, CA 93067
805-565-9463
800-249-9463
tastingroom@
summerlandwine.com
www.summerlandwine.com

OWNER: Nebil Zarif.

LOCATION: .25 mile east of U.S. 101.

APPELLATIONS: Edna Valley, Santa Maria Valley, Sta. Rita Hills, Paso Robles, Santa Ynez Valley.

HOURS: 11 A.M.–6 P.M. Tuesday–Sunday.

TASTINGS: $8 for 6 wines; $12 for 6 reserve wines (includes glass).

TOURS: None.

THE WINES: Cabernet Sauvignon, Chardonnay, Duet (Rhône blend), Grenache, Merlot, Orange Muscat, Petite Sirah, Pinot Gris, Pinot Noir, Rosé, Sauvignon Blanc, Syrah, Trio (Syrah, Grenache, Mourvèdre blend), Viognier, Zinfandel.

SPECIALTY: Vineyard-designated Pinot Noir.

WINEMAKER: Etienne Terlinden.

ANNUAL PRODUCTION: 25,000 cases.

OF SPECIAL NOTE: Gift shop with imported and local items, including linens, cushions, and music CDs. Outdoor patio overlooking Summerland village main avenue. Rosé and Port available only in tasting room.

NEARBY ATTRACTIONS: Summerland Beach; Carpinteria State Beach (swimming, camping); Lotusland (private botanic garden with public tours); Carpinteria Valley Museum of History (displays on native Chumash and early settlers).

ZACA MESA WINERY & VINEYARDS

ZACA MESA WINERY & VINEYARDS
6905 Foxen Canyon Rd.
Los Olivos, CA 93441
805-688-9339
800-350-7972
info@zacamesa.com
www.zacamesa.com

OWNERS: John and
Lou Cushman.

LOCATION: 7.4 miles north
of Hwy. 154.

APPELLATION: Santa Ynez
Valley.

HOURS: 10 A.M.–4 P.M. daily.

TASTINGS: $10 for 6 wines.

TOURS: None.

THE WINES: Chardonnay, Cinsault, Grenache, Mourvèdre, Roussanne, Syrah, Viognier, Z Blanc (Roussanne, Grenache Blanc, Viognier blend), Z Cuvée (Grenache, Mourvèdre, Syrah, Cinsaut blend, depending on vintage), Z Gris (rosé), Z Three (Syrah, Grenache, Mourvèdre blend).

SPECIALTY: Estate-grown
Syrah.

WINEMAKER: Eric Mohseni.

ANNUAL PRODUCTION:
35,000 cases.

OF SPECIAL NOTE: Grassy courtyard with picnic tables and life-size chessboard. Hiking trail rises to 1,500-foot elevation and spectacular views of Santa Ynez Valley.

NEARBY ATTRACTION:
Historic 1875 San Ramon Chapel (Benjamin Foxen Memorial Chapel).

The Foxen Canyon Wine Trail snakes its way for twenty miles through some of California's most scenic countryside. Near its midpoint, La Zaca encompasses a wild region, where deer, mountain lions, and even black bears still roam the hills. The native Chumash revered the site, calling it *zaca*, or "restful place."

In 1972 a group including twin brothers and real estate investors John and Lou Cushman purchased the 1,750-acre property, originally part of the 1830s Rancho La Zaca Mexican land grant. In 1973 they started the Zaca Mesa vineyard on soil that was once covered in prehistoric ocean dunes. Initial plantings included Cabernet Sauvignon, Chardonnay, Merlot, Zinfandel, Pinot Noir, and Riesling. The early fruit and vintages showed great promise, and in 1978 Zaca Mesa built a winery, which was expanded in 1981 into a twenty-thousand-square-foot complex with one of the region's first tasting rooms. That same year Zaca Mesa planted the first Syrah in Santa Barbara County, in a vineyard block that continues to provide low-yield grapes with intense flavor for the winery's coveted Black Bear Syrah. Many now-famous winemakers spent their early years at Zaca Mesa and later founded their own labels.

Zaca Mesa
ESTATE GROWN AND BOTTLED

SYRAH
SANTA YNEZ VALLEY
2005

Few other vineyards existed in the region in the early 1970s. Zaca Mesa experimented with grape varietals for twenty years to determine which grew best in the different microclimates and soils. This grape-growing experience determined Zaca Mesa's path from the 1990s onward: Rhône varietals prosper here, warmed by the sun early in the day and cooled by ocean breezes flowing through Los Alamos Valley to the vineyard from thirty miles away. The winery shifted its focus to Syrah and Rhône blends with great success. In 1995 *Wine Spectator* placed the 1993 Zaca Mesa Syrah sixth on its Top 100 Wines list.

Zaca Mesa now maintains 240 acres of vineyards, follows sustainable growing practices, and keeps all fruit for its own estate wines. The visitor center, a lofty cedar structure designed to fit into the surroundings, looks much the same as it did nearly thirty years ago: cedar floors, soaring two-story ceilings, and gifts, cheeses, olives, and crackers displayed atop oak barrels. A U-shaped tasting bar with an aged steel top and wood planks evokes the same rustic character as the original room. Outdoors, visitors are encouraged to sit in the grassy, oak-shaded courtyard, where they can play chess with life-size pieces on a wood board, picnic, and relax after hiking on the estate's scenic nature trail in ancient Chumash territory.

SAN LUIS
OBISPO
COUNTY

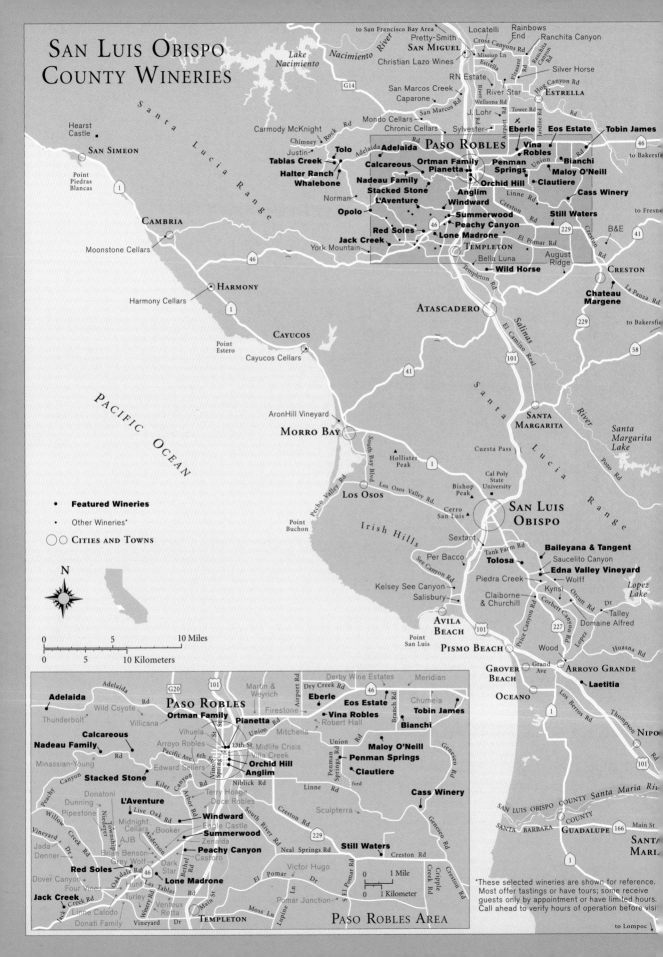

SAN LUIS OBISPO COUNTY WINERIES

Featured Wineries
· Other Wineries*
◯◯ **CITIES AND TOWNS**

N

0   5   10 Miles
0   5   10 Kilometers

Hearst Castle
SAN SIMEON
Point Piedras Blancas

Santa Lucia Range

PACIFIC OCEAN

CAMBRIA
Moonstone Cellars

HARMONY
Harmony Cellars

CAYUCOS
Point Estero
Cayucos Cellars

Point Buchon

Irish Hills

Los Osos Valley Rd.
LOS OSOS
Pecho Valley Rd.

South Bay Blvd
Hollister Peak
AronHill Vineyard
MORRO BAY

Bishop Peak
Cal Poly State University
Cerro San Luis
SAN LUIS OBISPO

Cuesta Pass
SANTA MARGARITA

Santa Margarita Lake

Sextant
Per Bacco
See Canyon Rd.
Kelsey See Canyon
Salisbury

Tank Farm Rd.
Baileyana & Tangent
Saucelito Canyon
Tolosa
Edna Valley Vineyard
Wolff
Piedra Creek
Kynsi
Orcutt Rd
Claiborne & Churchill
Talley
Domaine Alfred

Lopez Lake

AVILA BEACH
Point San Luis
PISMO BEACH

Wood
Grand Ave
GROVER BEACH
Arroyo Grande
Laetitia
OCEANO

Huasna Rd.
Los Berros Rd.
Thompson Rd
NIPO

ATASCADERO
Salinas River
El Camino Real

CRESTON
Chateau Margene
La Panza Rd

B&E

to San Francisco Bay Area
Pretty-Smith
SAN MIGUEL
Christian Lazo Wines

Locatelli
Cross Canyons Rd
Rainbows End
Ranchita Canyon
Mission Ln
Estrella
Silver Horse
RN Estate
River Star
ESTRELLA
to Bakersfield

San Marcos Creek
Caparone
San Marcos Rd
J. Lohr
Tower Rd
Eberle
Eos Estate
Tobin James

Carmody McKnight
Mondo Cellars
Chronic Cellars
Sylvester
PASO ROBLES
Vina Robles
Bianchi
Justin
Tolo
Adelaida
Ortman Family
Pianetta
Penman Springs
Maloy O'Neill
Tablas Creek
Calcareous
Orchid Hill
Clautiere
Halter Ranch
Nadeau Family
Anglim
Cass Winery
Whalebone
Stacked Stone
Windward
Linne Rd
Norman
L'Aventure
Summerwood
Creston Rd
Still Waters
Opolo
Peachy Canyon
El Pomar Rd
Red Soles
Lone Madrone
Jack Creek
York Mountain
TEMPLETON
Bella Luna
August Ridge
Wild Horse
Templeton Rd

to Fresno
to Bakersfield

*These selected wineries are shown for reference. Most offer tastings or have tours; some receive guests only by appointment or have limited hours. Call ahead to verify hours of operation before visi

PASO ROBLES AREA

Adelaida
Thunderbolt
Wild Coyote
Adelaida Rd
Villicana
PASO ROBLES
Ortman Family
Martin & Weyrich
Derby Wine Estates
Dry Creek Rd
Meridian

Calcareous
Minassian-Young
Nadeau Family
Stacked Stone
Donatoni
Dunning
Pipestone
Midnight Cellars
AJB
Brian Benson
Grey Wolf
Jada
Denner
Dover Canyon
Four Vines
Red Soles
Jack Creek
Linne Calodo
Donati Family
TEMPLETON

Pianetta
Eberle
Vina Robles
Eos Estate
Tobin James
Bianchi
Firestone
Robert Hall
Maloy O'Neill
Penman Springs
Clautiere
Cass Winery

Vihuela
Arroyo Robles
Pacific Ave
Edward Sellers
L'Aventure
Live Oak Rd
Booker
Eagle Castle
Windward
Summerwood
Peachy Canyon
Castoro
Lone Madrone
Still Waters
Sculpterra
Neal Springs Rd
Victor Hugo
Orchid Hill
Anglim
Niblick Rd
Terry Hoage
Zenaida
Midlife Crisis
Villa Creek

0   1 Mile
0   1 Kilometer

to Lompoc

SAN LUIS OBISPO COUNTY
SANTA BARBARA COUNTY
Santa Maria River
GUADALUPE
Main St
SANTA MARI

San Luis Obispo County is divided into two distinct growing regions by the Santa Lucia Range. Rising parallel to the coastline, the range separates the south, with its volcanic soils and mild, maritime climate, from the north, a region of fossil-studded soils and fifty-degree temperature swings. U.S. 101, running north-south through the county, crosses the range at Cuesta Grade, where coastal plains meet oak woodlands.

San Luis Obispo County drew international attention to its nascent wine industry in 1922, when renowned Polish pianist Ignace Paderewski planted Zin-  fandel near Paso Robles. The 1960s saw success with Pinot Noir on the west side of Paso Robles, and wine grapes began to replace cattle ranches and hot springs as the region's dominant fea- tures. The 1973 planting of Paragon Vineyard established Edna Valley, near the city of San Luis Obispo, as a prime grape-growing area. Since the early 1980s, vinicultural growth has exploded, especially in North County, the region north of Cuesta Grade, which is home to 75 percent of San Luis Obispo County's 230 wineries.

Along the coast, Highway 1 winds past Montaña de Oro State Park, Morro Bay, and Cambria, where art galleries and antique stores abound. North of Cambria, Hearst Castle sits regally on a hill overlooking the sea at San Simeon. Turning inland at Avila Beach, U.S. 101 curves past downtown San Luis Obispo, then heads over Cuesta Grade and into North County, which is dotted with lavender farms, alpaca ranches, and orchards.

Adelaida Cellars

Named for an historic mining community that once flourished in the hills west of Paso Robles, Adelaida Cellars has been producing wine since 1981, well before the region soared to viticultural prominence. Ten years after the winery's inception, founder John Munch, a pioneering winemaker and mentor to dozens of aspiring vintners, partnered with the Van Steenwyk family to expand the business and build a production facility on the family's sprawling walnut ranch.

Lying at the end of a long country driveway flanked by grapevines on one side, walnut trees on the other, the homey winery complex welcomes visitors with a shaded porch and lush lawn for picnicking. The tasting room door, which sports black stencils left over from its original incarnation as an oak cask, opens to reveal a stylish space with a view of barrels in the cellar at the opposite end of the room. Furnishings include a leather sofa, an antique ice box doubling as bookshelves, and tables displaying olive oil, jams, and wine accessories, as well as fresh walnuts and almonds from the orchards nearby. Behind the granite-topped tasting bar stretching the length of the room, windows that frame glimpses of stainless steel tanks and dozens of glistening wine bottles confirm the purpose of a visit. After greeting guests, well-trained staff members share entertaining anecdotes about local lore and history, as well as details about the wines they are pouring.

Don and Elizabeth Van Steenwyk became sole owners of the winery in 1999, after planting ten acres of Syrah and Cabernet Sauvignon, and acquiring the thirty-two-acre HMR Vineyard, originally installed by viticultural trailblazer Dr. Stanley Hoffman, in 1964, and containing the oldest Pinot Noir in San Luis Obispo County. Since then, the Van Steenwyks have planted a half-dozen more vineyard blocks, including thirty acres of Rhône varietals, eighteen acres of Zinfandel propagated from eighty-year-old heritage vines, and five acres of Muscat Blanc and Portuguese varietals for crafting dessert wines.

The couple originally bought their walnut ranch in the mid-1970s as an investment. They commuted to the property on weekends from their Southern California home, while Don built a career supplying electronic equipment to the oil industry and Elizabeth wrote children's books. Although both continue to ply their respective trades, Elizabeth's life now revolves around running the winery and tasting room, because, she jokes, she was the only one who didn't have a day job. Each fall, the family brings in a half-million pounds of walnuts from eight hundred acres of trees, but not before harvesting the high-quality wine grapes that made the region famous.

ADELAIDA CELLARS
5805 Adelaida Rd.
Paso Robles, CA 93446
805-239-8980
wines@adelaida.com
www.adelaida.com

OWNERS: Van Steenwyk family.

LOCATION: 7 miles west of downtown Paso Robles.

APPELLATION: Paso Robles.

HOURS: 10 A.M.–5 P.M. daily.

TASTINGS: $10 for 6 wines (applicable to purchase).

TOURS: On weekends.

THE WINES: Cabernet Sauvignon, Chardonnay, Chenin Blanc, Nebbiolo, Pinot Noir, Sangiovese, Syrah, Viognier, Zinfandel.

SPECIALTIES: Ice Wine (Muscat/Viognier dessert wine), Version (red Rhône blend: Mourvèdre, Grenache, Counoise, Cinsault), Version (white Rhône blend: Grenache Blanc, Roussanne).

WINEMAKER: Terry Culton.

ANNUAL PRODUCTION: 15,000 cases.

OF SPECIAL NOTE: Lawn and shaded porch for picnicking. Wine accessories, olive oil, and local almonds and walnuts sold in tasting room. Summer brunches and bimonthly library tastings; barrel tasting by appointment.

NEARBY ATTRACTION: Mt. Olive Organic Farm (tours, olive and olive oil tasting).

ANGLIM WINERY

ANGLIM WINERY
740 Pine St.
Paso Robles, CA 93446
805-227-6813
info@anglimwinery.com
www.anglimwinery.com

OWNERS: Steve and
Steffanie Anglim.

LOCATION: Downtown
Paso Robles.

APPELLATION: Paso Robles.

HOURS: 11 A.M.–6 P.M.
Thursday–Monday, except
noon–6 P.M. Sunday, and
by appointment.

TASTINGS: Complimentary
for standard tastings. $5
for 4–6 reserve wines.

TOURS: Winery tour
and barrel tasting by
appointment.

THE WINES: Cabernet
Sauvignon, Grenache,
Pinot Noir, Rhône blends,
Roussanne, Syrah,
Viognier, Zinfandel.

SPECIALTIES: Rhône varieties and blends.

WINEMAKER: Steve Anglim.

ANNUAL PRODUCTION:
3,500 cases.

OF SPECIAL NOTE: Tasting
room is the starting
point for a walking tour
of historic Paso Robles
buildings.

NEARBY ATTRACTION:
Paso Robles City Park
(site of festivals, summer
concerts, farmers market).

The circular, tree-lined driveway leading to the Anglim Winery tasting room kindles a nostalgic sense of Main Street U.S.A., where shopkeepers prop open their doors, locals visit along shady sidewalks, and passenger trains glide into an adjacent Amtrak station twice daily. Housed in a restored 122-year-old building that served as the station's original depot, the tasting room offers a bright, airy space in which to sample food-friendly wines made from grapes grown all over San Luis Obispo and Santa Barbara counties. Single-vineyard offerings showcase the flavors of a particular site, and the rest of the Rhône-inspired lineup provides a sensory tour of the region's diverse fruit. Sipping on the quiet back patio or at the granite-topped counter, visitors can watch the dog walkers and travelers who animate the rail-side scene. Tall windows illuminate century-old nicks in the hardwood floor, and bead-board and chair rails lend period authenticity to interior walls. An antique cabinet still bearing cubbyhole labels, one dated 1904, reveals its long-ago service in the rail office.

Anglim

2005
BEST BARREL BLEND
45% MOURVEDRE, 45% SYRAH
10% GRENACHE
PASO ROBLES

Steve and Steffanie Anglim opened their tasting room in 2005 to help foster direct sales and tie the label to a specific spot. They chose the depot not only for its relaxed ambience and key role in local history, but also because it provided enough space for an office and a play area for the couple's four-year-old daughter.

The Anglims first came to viniculture in 1996, while in the midst of successful careers in corporate finance and management consulting, respectively, when Steve received a winemaking kit as a gag gift. The resulting wine was deemed "disgusting," but the experience inspired the pair to gather bins and barrels in their garage to make the real thing. After extensive reading, courses at UC Davis, and six years of experimentation, they crushed a little Syrah and Viognier in 2002, and launched the family business with the release of their first commercial wine in 2004. With technical advice from the region's generous winemakers, the Anglims have expanded their portfolio to include nearly a dozen varietals and blends. Today, Steve makes wine at a shared-use facility that caters to small producers. He keeps output consistent, unless an extra ton or two of irresistible fruit comes along to boost the yield.

Until the pair plants their own fruit, Steffanie figures that the two potted grapevines on the patio qualify as their estate vineyard. With a cheerful tasting room and grapevines in sight, as well as bus, rail, and rental car service available next door, Anglim Winery may be the ideal place to begin a tour of Paso Robles wine country.

BAILEYANA & TANGENT WINERIES

I n 1909 the rural Edna Valley farming community built the Independence Schoolhouse near the peak of Islay Hill, the seventh in a string of volcanic plugs that stretches across southern San Luis Obispo County. Local children attended the one-room school until it closed in 1956. In 2003 the restored historic yellow schoolhouse reopened to welcome students of a different type—those who come to learn about Baileyana & Tangent wines.

The story of Baileyana & Tangent Wineries begins with Catharine Niven and her husband, Jack, who shared a passion for wine. They were living in Northern California at the time, but Catharine, who grew up on a Kentucky thoroughbred horse farm, yearned to relocate to a more rural region. The couple decided in the early 1970s to move to San Luis Obispo, where they could pursue their winemaking dreams. They purchased a promising piece of property with volcanic soils in the Edna Valley and founded Paragon Vineyard, where Jack pioneered the planting of the first commercial grapevines in the area. Jack focused on the large-scale vineyard, and after they completed their new home in

the Edna Valley, Catharine experimented with a 3.5-acre parcel in her front yard. Her Burgundian-style, tightly spaced rows with vertical canopies produced excellent grapes, so she created Baileyana Winery in the 1980s, named after the Northern California neighborhood where she first met Jack.

Sons Jim and John Niven eventually took over the winery. They acquired property at the base of Islay Hill and planted Firepeak Vineyard with Chardonnay, Pinot Noir, and Syrah. Catharine's grandsons, Michael and John, joined the team in the late 1990s, and in 1998 the family hired veteran French winemaker Christian Roguenant, formerly head enologist for the famed Champagne Deutz and an expert in Pinot Noir and Chardonnay. The Nivens gave Roguenant a blank slate to design a high-tech winery that would produce exceptional wines from estate grapes. Under the Baileyana Winery label, Roguenant transforms Firepeak Vineyard fruit into premium Pinot Noir, Syrah, and Chardonnay. A sister label, Tangent Winery, showcases white wines (apart from Chardonnay) made mostly from grapes grown in the Paragon Vineyard, source of uncommon varietals such as Albariño and Grüner Veltliner.

Visitors can sample the wines at the tasting bar inside the old schoolhouse. Flower gardens, olive trees, and an outdoor patio surround the pretty yellow building. The Independence Schoolhouse turned a century old in 2009, and Roguenant has made two special sparkling white wines, Cuvée 1909, to celebrate the anniversary of the beloved Edna Valley landmark.

BAILEYANA & TANGENT WINERIES
5828 Orcutt Rd.
San Luis Obispo, CA 93401
805-269-8200
info@baileyana.com
www.baileyana-tangent.com

OWNERS: Niven family.

LOCATION: 6 miles southeast of downtown San Luis Obispo.

APPELLATION: Edna Valley.

HOURS: 10 A.M.–5 P.M. daily.

TASTINGS: $5 for 5 wines.

TOURS: None.

THE WINES: Albariño, Chardonnay, Pinot Blanc, Pinot Gris, Pinot Noir, Riesling, Sauvignon Blanc, Syrah, Viognier.

SPECIALTIES: Albariño, Chardonnay, Pinot Gris, Pinot Noir, Sauvignon Blanc, Syrah.

WINEMAKER: Christian Roguenant.

ANNUAL PRODUCTION: 29,000 cases.

OF SPECIAL NOTE: Gourmet marketplace items and gifts available in tasting room. Picnic grounds and bocce ball courts on-site. Baileyana block-specific Pinot Noir and Chardonnay and Tangent Riesling available only in tasting room.

NEARBY ATTRACTIONS: Mission San Luis Obispo de Tolosa; San Luis Obispo County Historical Museum and other historic buildings in downtown San Luis Obispo; Pismo State Beach (swimming, hiking, camping).

BIANCHI WINERY & TASTING ROOM

**BIANCHI WINERY &
TASTING ROOM**
3380 Branch Rd.
Paso Robles, CA 93446
805-226-9922
info@bianchiwine.com
www.bianchiwine.com

OWNER: Glenn Bianchi.

LOCATION: 6 miles east of
downtown Paso Robles.

APPELLATION: Paso Robles.

HOURS: 10 A.M.–5 P.M. daily.

TASTINGS: $5 for 7 wines.
Reservations recommended
for groups of 10 or more.

TOURS: By appointment.

THE WINES: Barbera,
Cabernet Franc, Cabernet
Sauvignon, Chardonnay,
Merlot, Muscat Canelli,
Negrette, Petite Sirah, Pinot
Grigio, Pinot Noir, Refosco,
Sangiovese, Sauvignon
Blanc, Syrah, Zinfandel.

SPECIALTIES: Cabernet
Sauvignon, Syrah, Merlot,
Zen Ranch Zinfandel.

WINEMAKER: Tom Lane.

ANNUAL PRODUCTION:
12,000 cases.

OF SPECIAL NOTE: Deli foods
sold in tasting room. Gift
shop with clothing, pottery,
and wine accessories. Vineyard House, a renovated
farmhouse, offers overnight
lodging. Wines including
Barbera, Cabernet Franc,
Muscat Canelli, Refosco,
and Sangiovese available
only in tasting room.

NEARBY ATTRACTIONS:
Barney Schwartz Park
(lake, picnic areas);
Estrella Warbird Museum
(restored military aircraft,
memorabilia).

The rural road that leads to the Bianchi estate in the bucolic Paso Robles countryside traverses a series of oak-studded rolling hills, blanketed by vineyards, row crops, and pastures. Suddenly, as visitors drive through the estate entrance, an oasis rises amid the undulating knolls: a waterfall-fed lake and a striking complex of modern structures. Migrating birds skim across the water next to a lakeside deck, stone terraces, and a dramatic visitor center—a contemporary interpretation of an old California mission in adobe, wood, and stone. A stunning green-toned winery facility with a corrugated tin roof sits on a gentle rise a short walk from the visitor center. This serene, water-oriented scene reflects owner Glenn Bianchi's desire to create not just a winery and hospitality center, but an attractive destination where travelers can take a break and enjoy the natural setting.

The Bianchi family's involvement in the wine industry dates to 1974, when Glenn and his father, Joseph, invested in a winery and vineyard on the banks of the San Joaquin River in the Central Valley. The business grew into a large-scale producer of wines for the general consumer. In the late 1990s, Glenn actively pursued a longtime dream of finding a place where he could grow world-class wines. After a statewide search for a vineyard site, he settled on Paso Robles, impressed by the caliber of the regional wines and by the pristine natural landscapes. In January 2000, Bianchi purchased a forty-acre property on the east side of Paso Robles. Sparing no expense, he soon began construction of the visitor center and a state-of-the-art winery with computer-controlled fermentation tanks, and developed a small pond into a scenic lake. In the twenty-acre vineyard, he replanted the existing Cabernet vines and added Syrah, Merlot, and Zinfandel varietals. Winemaker Tom Lane, who has more than two decades of winemaking experience, joined Bianchi as director of winemaking in 2005. He crafts ultrapremium wines from estate fruit and selects high-quality grapes (mostly Italian varietals) from other Central Coast growers to create an array of small-lot wines.

The visitor center blends modern design elements with traditional materials. Glass walls soar up toward cathedral ceilings with metal beams, stainless steel and glass accents adorn the maple tasting bar and display cabinets, and a stone fireplace fronts a comfortable lounge area with dark red leather and cherrywood furniture. The center extends outdoors to a spacious deck overlooking the lake and vineyards, where guests are invited to enjoy Bianchi wines, observe the wildlife, and relax to the soothing sounds of the waterfall and cooling breezes from the lake.

CALCAREOUS VINEYARD

The owners and staff at Calcareous Vineyard invite visitors to come for the wine and stay for the sense of place, a compelling offer of liquid art and authentic landscape. Named after the chalky soil that distinguishes its west side *terroir*, the hilltop winery features a thick lawn dotted with tables and chairs, an official bocce ball court, and a stunning panorama of hills, oaks, and sky. With glass walls made of accordion doors that can be collapsed to admit air and even more light, the tasting room serves as a fitting showcase for both the lush wines and the site's considerable attributes.

Inside, stone pillars contrast with the mahogany hues of the open-beamed ceiling and tasting bar, and the open floor space allows plenty of room for mingling with other tasters, browsing the

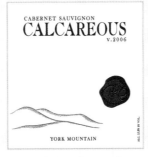

display tables, or catching the endless view. The tasting room opened in 2008, after a smaller one in the winery proved to be too limited, and was named Lloyd's Lookout, in honor of Lloyd Messer, the winery's visionary cofounder. Messer was a traveling man whose Iowa-based beer and wine distributing business frequently brought him to Paso Robles, where he enjoyed rubbing elbows with area winemakers and dreaming about a different kind of life. When he sold his business to become a grape grower in the late 1990s, he asked his daughter, Dana Brown, to join him as a partner. Brown, who had started a wine distributorship after college, was ready for a career change after having her first child. She caught her dad's enthusiasm, sold her business, and headed west.

In 2000 the pair purchased nearly eight hundred acres of land, but not before securing fruit for the winery's 1999 debut vintage of Chardonnay and Pinot Noir. Eager and impatient, they planted a twenty-five-acre vineyard and continued to make wine at neighboring facilities with purchased fruit, until opening their own winery in March 2006. When their vineyard began producing, they dedicated the Calcareous label to their estate program, and Twisted Sisters, a label wryly named for Brown and her younger sister, Erika Messer, to wines made from nonestate fruit.

Since Lloyd's sudden death in May 2006, Brown and Messer have shouldered the details of the business. The sisters continue to build the brand and celebrate his daring dream. Atop a chunk of calcareous soil in a flowerbed beside the tasting room, they have placed a bronzed pair of Lloyd's old work boots, a loving tribute to the man whose vision started it all.

CALCAREOUS VINEYARD
3430 Peachy Canyon Rd.
Paso Robles, CA 93446
805-239-0289
service@calcareous.com
www.calcareous.com

OWNERS: Dana Brown, Erika Messer.

LOCATION: 3 miles west of downtown Paso Robles.

APPELLATION: Paso Robles.

HOURS: 11 A.M.–5 P.M. daily.

TASTINGS: $5 for 6–8 wines.

TOURS: By appointment.

THE WINES: Cabernet Sauvignon, Chardonnay, Petit Verdot, Pinot Noir, Roussanne, Syrah, Viognier, Zinfandel.

SPECIALTIES: Tres Violet (Mourvèdre, Syrah, Grenache blend), Twisted Sisters Meritage.

WINEMAKER: Damian Grindley.

ANNUAL PRODUCTION: 10,500 cases.

OF SPECIAL NOTE: Picnic area with tables; bocce ball court. Wine-and-cheese pairings are available on request ($12); on-site kitchen offers light lunches on weekends. Gift shop stocks books, wine accessories, and light snacks.

NEARBY ATTRACTION: Paso Robles City Park (site of festivals, summer concerts, farmers market).

CASS WINERY

CASS WINERY
7350 Linne Rd.
Paso Robles, CA 93446
805-239-1730
info@casswines.com
www.casswines.com

OWNERS: Steve Cass,
Ted Plemons.

LOCATION: 7.2 miles east
of U.S. 101.

APPELLATION: Paso Robles.

HOURS: Noon–5 P.M.
Monday–Friday;
11 A.M.–6 P.M. Saturday
and Sunday.

TASTINGS: $10 for 7 wines.

TOURS: On request.

THE WINES: Cabernet Franc,
Cabernet Sauvignon,
Grenache, Marsanne,
Mourvèdre, Petite Sirah,
Roussanne, Syrah, Viognier.

SPECIALTY: Rockin' One
(Syrah, Mourvèdre, Petite
Sirah, Grenache blend).

WINEMAKER: Lood Kotze.

ANNUAL PRODUCTION:
5,000 cases.

OF SPECIAL NOTE: Wines are
100 percent estate grown.
On-site café serves gourmet
lunch daily 12–4 P.M. or by
reservation. Cooking classes
offered. Annual grape
stomp and piano concert
held in the fall.

NEARBY ATTRACTIONS:
Barney Schwartz Park
(lake, picnic areas);
Estrella Warbird Museum
(restored military aircraft,
memorabilia).

Located at a country crossroads way off the beaten path, Cass Winery emerges like a lush mirage from among the alluvial hills east of Paso Robles. Bracketed by a 146-acre vineyard is a cream-colored winery and tasting room. Splashes of outdoor art, including a vintage railroad bell, old basket press, and flying angel weathervane, dot the grounds. Spreading oaks shade a rustic seating area. In front of the tasting room, tables and chairs make for a quiet retreat or picnic spot under a vine-entwined shelter.

Inside, visitors taste an array of estate wines, predominantly red Rhônes, poured on most days by Kristen Cass, daughter of Steve Cass, one of the winery's founding partners. Near the eye-catching silver tasting bar built of industrial diamond plate, glass doors framed by the rim of a giant cask afford a view into the barrel room. Colorful paintings hang in front of an impromptu col- lage crafted from corks, and in a softly lit space opposite, an informal café, complete with commercial kitchen and executive chef, serves a gour- met lunch daily. Specialties include truffle pizza, crab cakes, and Cuban pork sandwiches, inviting fare for hungry travelers exploring what neighborhood producers call the Backroads Wineries.

Steve Cass and his business partner, Ted Plemons, who owns a local construction company, opened the winery in 2005 after falling under the spell of Rhône wines while on a trip to South Africa. They decided that they could grow comparable fruit in Paso Robles and were among the first growers in the United States to buy grapevines through ENTAV (Establissement National Technique pour l'Amélioration de la Viticulture), a French agency that field-tests plant material for health and vinicultural suitability. Cass credits the certified vines with his vineyard's uniform ripening, consistent quality, and immediate success.

Cass and Plemons hired South African winemaker Lood Kotze to craft wines similar to the ones they encountered on their trip. Under Kotze's skilled supervision, the wines have borne out their hunch about the region's potential to produce superior Rhônes and proven to be a mighty draw for wine lovers. Most arrive by car or bicycle to taste the wines and tuck into lunch, but more than one local has turned into the winery on horseback, making the stop while on a leisurely ride. The partners continue to sell 80 percent of their grapes to other California wineries, and they are delighted to have a cellar full of their favorite Rhône-style wines, grown and bottled in Paso Robles.

CHATEAU MARGENE

Determined to make Cabernet Sauvignon to rival the benchmark vintages of Napa Valley, Mike and Margene Mooney spent eight years seeking vineyard property in California before discovering the Paso Robles appellation. Amid the rolling, oak-studded hills of the appellation's east side, they found a distinctive region with the lean soil, deep water, summer heat, and afternoon sea breezes ideal for ripening the Bordeaux varietals they wanted to grow. In 1998 the Mooneys purchased twenty-two acres near Creston and founded Chateau Margene, which is located on the appellation's extreme southeast side. The couple planted a six-acre vineyard near the front of their property, where the lush vines now greet visitors passing through the winery's swinging, farm-style gate.

An unpaved road curves beneath mature redwoods, oaks, and pines, past a turn-of-the-century farmhouse, barn, and shady corral, where two horses nod a lazy hello, and ends beside a decorative chicken coop flanked by flower-filled gardens. Just beyond stands the winery, a dusty white, porticoed structure the Mooneys built in 2001 to double as a production facility and spacious tasting room.

Here, visitors stepping into the cool half-light find aromatic oak barrels stacked to the ceiling and a friendly member of the Mooney clan—if not Mike or Margene, then one of their two sons—ready to pour wines bottled under the Chateau Margene and recently launched Mooney Family labels. Visible through glass doors, an expanse of green lawn meets a shady, sofa-lined deck, lending the relaxed feel of a rural resort as tasters explore the wines produced by what Mooney describes as "a house of reds."

Mooney is a seventh-generation Californian whose forefathers were part of Juan Bautista de Anza's expedition that colonized the state in 1776. He left a career in business so that he and Margene could take on the challenge of planting a vineyard and starting a winery that would produce world-class Cabernet Sauvignon and Bordeaux varietals. Lacking formal education in viticulture or enology, they solicited the help of two local consultants. Through the 1999 vintage, this sage advice helped the couple gain the knowledge and experience to develop their own style of crafting rich, bold wines.

In 2003 Chateau Margene made headlines when the winery's 2000 Cabernet Sauvignon won first place at the Cabernet Sauvignon Shootout, cosponsored by *Wine Enthusiast Magazine*, in a double-blind tasting of 311 international entries judged by consumers, industry panelists, and members of the wine trade. That vintage sold out immediately, setting the pace for subsequent Chateau Margene vintages and confirming the stellar potential of Paso Robles Cabernet Sauvignon.

CHATEAU MARGENE
4385 La Panza Rd.
Creston, CA 93432
805-238-2321
info@chateaumargene.com
www.chateaumargene.com

OWNERS: Michael and Margene Mooney.

LOCATION: 15 miles east of Atascadero and southeast of Paso Robles, 2.2 miles east of Hwy. 41.

APPELLATION: Paso Robles.

HOURS: Noon–5 P.M. Friday–Sunday. Closed holidays.

TASTINGS: $10 for 5 wines (applicable to purchase); reserve tasting by appointment.

TOURS: By appointment.

THE WINES: Cabernet Franc, Cabernet Sauvignon, GSM (Rhône blend), Petite Sirah, Pinot Noir.

SPECIALTIES: Beau Mélange, Cielo Rosso.

WINEMAKER: Michael Mooney.

ANNUAL PRODUCTION: 3,000 cases.

OF SPECIAL NOTE: New Release Party (third Saturday in April). Viewing deck, shaded picnic area, beautiful lawn and gardens.

NEARBY ATTRACTION: Town of Creston (country store, Friday night barbecue, September rodeo).

CLAUTIERE VINEYARD

CLAUTIERE VINEYARD
1340 Penman Springs Rd.
Paso Robles, CA 93446
805-237-3789
info@clautiere.com
www.clautiere.com

OWNERS: Terry Brady,
Claudine Blackwell.

LOCATION: 6 miles east of
downtown Paso Robles.

APPELLATION: Paso Robles.

HOURS: Noon–5 P.M. daily.

TASTINGS: $5 for 6 wines
(applicable to purchase).

TOURS: None.

THE WINES: Cabernet
Sauvignon, Grand Rouge
(red blend), Grenache,
Mourvèdre, port, Rous-
sanne, Syrah, Viognier.

SPECIALTIES: Mon Beau
Rouge (Syrah, Counoise,
Grenache, Mourvèdre
blend), Mon Rouge
(Cabernet, Syrah blend).

WINEMAKERS: Terry Brady,
Matt Wilson.

ANNUAL PRODUCTION:
5,000 cases.

OF SPECIAL NOTE: Winery
has Zen rock garden and
other unusual landscape
features, plus a grassy
picnic area with tables.
Grand Rouge (red blend)
and Sweet Roussanne
available only in tasting
room.

NEARBY ATTRACTIONS:
Barney Schwartz Park
(lake, picnic areas);
Estrella Warbird Museum
(restored military aircraft,
memorabilia).

Art and wine mingle with playful wigs and wackiness at Clautiere Vineyard, one of the most unusual wine-touring destinations anywhere. After discovering a passion for wine during a trip to Portugal, Los Angeles restaurateurs Claudine Blackwell and Terry Brady headed to Paso Robles to start a vineyard and winery. In 1999 the couple purchased a 145-acre ranch planted in the 1980s with Cabernet Sauvignon and Rhône varietals. Brady, who had never made wine, quickly embarked on a self-taught farming and winemaking crash course with expert advisors John Munch and Matt Trevison, both established Paso Robles winemakers. Blackwell, an artist and designer, chan-neled her energies into transforming the property into a showcase for her creative expression.

Today the combination of fine wine and vibrant atmosphere has made Clautiere one of the region's most popular tasting rooms. At first glance, the dark red farmhouse off a bumpy country road blends in with

the rural landscape. But a closer look reveals signs of the quirkiness within. A stylish, 230-foot metal fence and shiny mosaic pillars mark the entrance to the winery; Blackwell handcrafted these and nearly every work of art on the premises. Mosaic and metal cubes of varying sizes hang from the limbs of an ancient oak and adorn the garden beneath. A series of mosaic spheres embellishes a second oak tree and garden across the yard. The brightly colored interior of the converted fifty-year-old farmhouse reflects an atmosphere similar to a French cabaret with zany elements. It has a black-and-white checkered floor, purple-periwinkle-silver color schemes, bright green window sashes, and harlequin accents throughout. Guests are encouraged to don colorful, madcap wigs and hats from Blackwell-designed hat boxes. Bewigged visitors often wander along gravel paths through the grounds, which include a carnival-style Hall of Mirrors outbuilding, a Zen rock garden, a barn converted into a cabaret-style theater (site of occasional themed costume parties), and the winery production facility. A solar system powers the entire winery complex.

Clautiere's setting may seem frivolous, but its bold, flavorful wines, particularly the Mon Beau Rouge blend, have earned serious awards. Brady crafts them with master blender Matt Wilson, whose two decades of experience include stints under John Falcone of Rusack Vineyards and Don Brady of Robert Hall. All wines are made from Clautiere's fifty-seven-acre estate vineyard, planted with Bordeaux and Rhône-style grapes, plus Portuguese varietals used to make a classic port wine. At the tasting bar, guests sample Clautiere wines, poured by a friendly and knowledgeable host—perhaps the only conventional aspect of a visit to this remarkable, multifaceted estate.

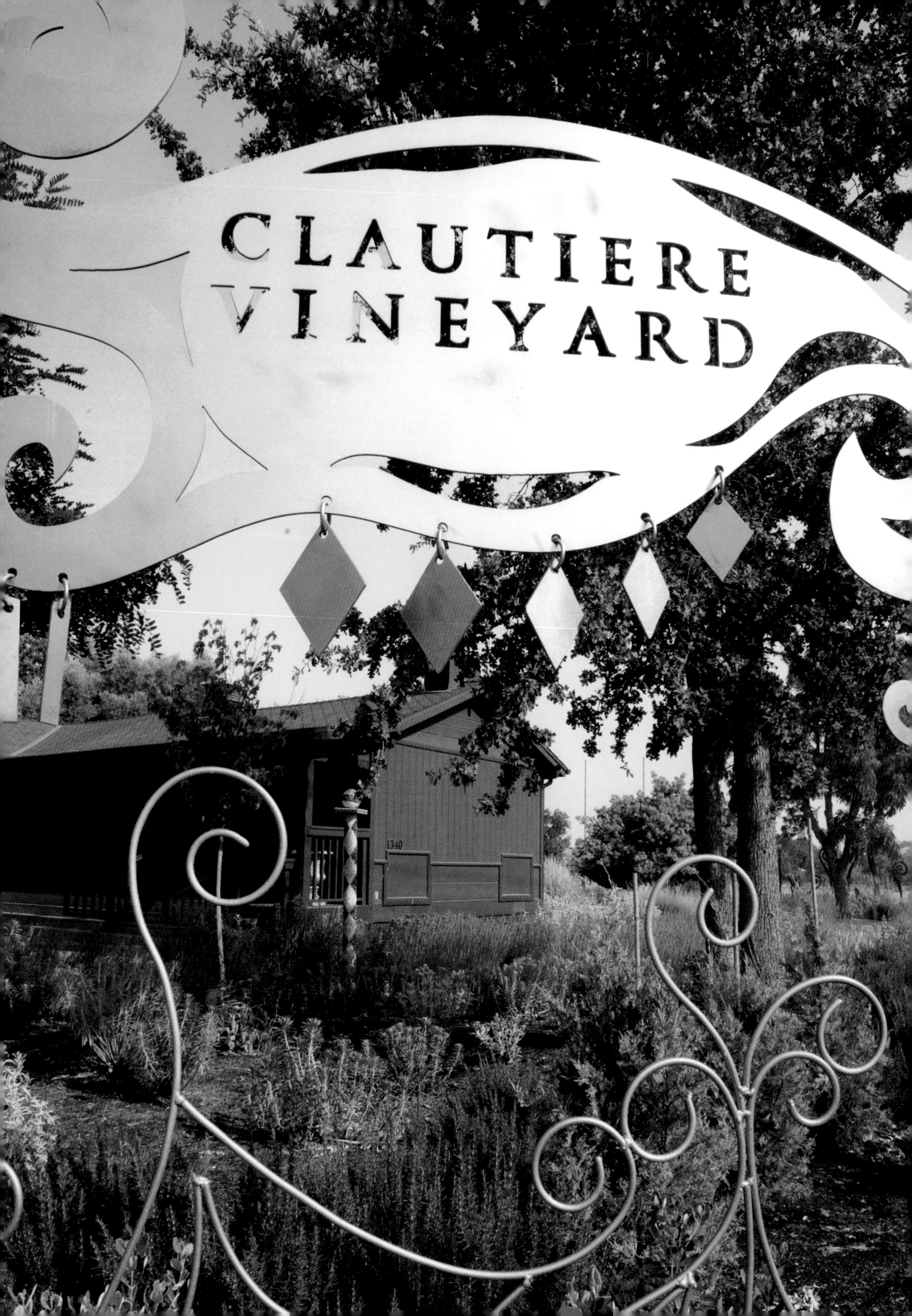
CLAUTIERE
VINEYARD
1340

EBERLE WINERY

In Paso Robles, the name Eberle conjures two iconic figures: pioneering winemaker Gary Eberle, who planted the region's first Syrah vines and helped establish Paso Robles as a premier winegrowing region, and the small statue of a wild boar, the mascot of Eberle Winery. *Eberle* means "small boar" in German, and images of wild boars appear on the winery logo. A bronze boar, cast by Baroque master Pietro Tacca in 1620, sits at the winery entrance. *Il Porcellino*, a replica of the marble boar that once stood in the Uffizi in Florence, invites visitors to rub its snout and toss coins in the fountain beneath its feet—a Florentine tradition said to bring good luck.

This good fortune is most sive oak tasting bar, where sam-at no charge, a rarity in the of free guided tours through the caves beneath the visitor center. tastings reflect Gary Eberle's about all aspects of winemaking tion to the bottles of wine they

readily apparent at the expan-ples of Eberle wines are poured region. It also comes in the form sixteen thousand square feet of The complimentary tours and firm belief in educating visitors so they form a personal connec-enjoy at the table.

Eberle's passion for wine, Cabernet Sauvignon in particular, developed when he was a doctoral student in cellular genetics at Louisiana State University. He decided he would rather be a winemaker and transferred to the enology doctoral program at UC Davis. In the early 1970s, he and his professors made a few pilgrimages to Paso Robles to collect soil samples, and their research pinpointed Paso Robles as an area of great grape-growing promise. He moved there to cofound Estrella River Winery (now Meridian) and worked as head winemaker for nearly a decade. He planted Syrah vines in 1974—the first in the United States since the repeal of Prohibition—and was the first Paso Robles winemaker to make a 100 percent Syrah wine. Eberle officially established his own label and winery partnership in 1982, purchasing sixty-five acres just a few miles west of Estrella River Winery. That year he released his flagship wine, the 1979 Cabernet Sauvignon. He also helped establish the Paso Robles appellation and completed a utilitarian cedar winery building.

The Eberle estate vineyard now produces Cabernet, Chardonnay, and Muscat Canelli grapes exclusively for Eberle wines. Eberle also has a partnership in nearby Mill Road and Steinbeck vineyards, which retain 20 percent of the harvest for Eberle wines and sell the remainder to other vintners. Over the decades, Eberle wines have earned more than three hundred gold medals, many of which are on display in the spacious California ranch–style visitor center overlooking one of Paso Robles's oldest and most legendary vineyards.

EBERLE WINERY
3810 Hwy. 46 East
Paso Robles, CA 93446
805-238-9607
tastingroom@eberlewinery.com
www.eberlewinery.com

OWNER/GENERAL PARTNER: Gary Eberle.

LOCATION: 3.5 miles east of U.S. 101.

APPELLATION: Paso Robles.

HOURS: 10 A.M.–5 P.M. daily in winter; 10 A.M.–6 P.M. daily in summer.

TASTINGS: Complimentary for 5 wines.

TOURS: Free guided cave tours every half hour daily. VIP tours ($25) include reserve tasting; reservations required.

THE WINES: Barbera, Cabernet Sauvignon, Chardonnay, Muscat Canelli, Sangiovese, Syrah, Viognier, Zinfandel.

SPECIALTIES: Vineyard-designated Cabernet Sauvignon and Syrah.

WINEMAKER: Ben Mayo.

ANNUAL PRODUCTION: 30,000 cases.

OF SPECIAL NOTE: Extensive wine caves available for touring. Monthly guest chef dinners in caves. Picnic deck overlooking vineyard; on-site bocce ball court. Gift shop offering ceramic ware, wine and food books, gourmet foods, and clothing. One-third of the winery's production, including library reserve wines, available only in tasting room.

NEARBY ATTRACTIONS: Paso Robles City Park (site of festivals, summer concerts, farmers market); Estrella Warbird Museum (restored military aircraft, memorabilia).

EDNA VALLEY VINEYARD

EDNA VALLEY VINEYARD
2585 Biddle Ranch Rd.
San Luis Obispo, CA 93401
805-544-5855
evvinfo@ednavalley.com
www.ednavalleyvineyard.
com

OWNERS: Diageo Chateau
and Estate Wines, and
Niven family.

LOCATION: 3 miles southeast
of San Luis Obispo Airport.

APPELLATION: Edna Valley.

HOURS: 10 A.M.–5 P.M. daily.

TASTINGS: $5 for 5 wines;
$10 for 5 limited-
production wines.

TOURS: Weekends, 11 A.M.–
3 P.M. on the hour. Reservations required for large
groups.

THE WINES: Cabernet
Sauvignon, Chardonnay,
Grenache, Merlot, Mourvè-
dre, Orange Muscat, Petite
Sirah, Pinot Gris, Pinot
Noir, Sauvignon Blanc,
Syrah, Viognier.

SPECIALTIES: Chardonnay,
Pinot Noir.

WINEMAKER: Harry Hansen.

ANNUAL PRODUCTION:
Unavailable.

OF SPECIAL NOTE: Edna
Valley Vineyard's estate
vineyard is one of the
oldest in the region. A
demonstration vineyard
features 14 varietals and
various trellising systems.
Tasting room includes
gourmet gift shop.

NEARBY ATTRACTIONS:
Mission San Luis Obispo
de Tolosa; San Luis Obispo
County Historical Museum
and other historic build-
ings in downtown San
Luis Obispo; Pismo State
Beach (swimming, hiking,
camping).

One of San Luis Obispo's oldest commercial plantings of wine grapes, Edna Valley Vine-yard's eleven hundred acres comprise more than half of the fruit growing in the Edna Valley appellation. The appellation was approved in 1982, a full two years after the Niven family partnered with the Napa-based Chalone Wine Group to establish Edna Valley Vineyard. The late Jack and Catharine Niven, who once headed a chain of more than a hundred Northern California grocery stores, turned to grape growing in 1973, when they planted the seminal Paragon Vineyard, which now serves as the winery's estate vineyard. The Nivens family's bold move proved the viticultural potential of south San Luis Obispo County and helped jump-start the wine industry that would eventually dominate the eight-mile-long Edna Valley.

Open to the nearby Pacific Ocean, the east/west-oriented valley enjoys a maritime climate of cool summers and warm winters that triggers Chardonnay to leaf out in February, while allowing Syrah to remain on the vine until late into November. This long growing season, as well as the soil's mix of marine sediment and vol-canic material, contributes to the unique flavors— from an unusual peach-pear dynamic in Chardonnay to a dark spice in Syrah—that distinguish the valley's singular fruit.

Winemaker Harry Hansen took the reins at Edna Valley Vineyard in 2001, after spending fifteen years in Sonoma County making sparkling wine and conducting vineyard trials. As an incentive for visitors to stop by the winery's stunning Jack Niven Hospitality Center, he crafts thirteen offerings exclusively for sale in the tasting room, located amid sweeping lawns and vineyards that stretch to the horizon. Unveiled in 1997, the center includes a fully stocked gourmet gift shop and a wall-to-wall tasting counter backed by a jaw-dropping view of foothills, grapevines, and ancient volcanoes pushing up from the valley floor. Weekend tasters eager to get a glimpse behind the scenes can tour the winery and barrel room, where cellar operations are often in full swing. During harvest, they may even see grapes rolling in by the truckload and fresh juice flowing from the press.

In 2005 Diageo Chateau and Estate Wines purchased the property and began replanting parts of the vineyard to take advantage of new clones and trellising systems. Just outside the tasting room, a demonstration vineyard boasting fourteen rows and as many different varietals and trellising options offers a detailed look at the elegant crop that made Edna Valley famous.

EOS ESTATE WINERY

Eos Estate Winery uses state-of-the-art, eco-friendly technology to harness the sun's energy to craft premium wines. Visits to the spacious, Italianate hospitality center, perched on a hilltop amid rose gardens in the heart of Paso Robles wine country, blend wine tasting with interactive learning experiences related to the estate's unusual, large-scale solar-powered winemaking and tasting room operations.

In 2007 Sapphire Wines acquired Eos Estate winery and sixty of its original vineyard acres. Sapphire is led by CEO Jeff Hopmayer, a successful wine and spirits entrepreneur who founded Original American Scones, which supplied various baked goods to Starbucks Coffee worldwide. A passionate supporter of eco-friendly wine production, Hopmayer launched a $5 million project to install a cutting-edge solar system to power the winery and tasting room operations. More than two acres of ground-mounted tracking solar arrays will supply all electrical power for the winery and tasting room. Additional roof-mounted solar arrays provide all water-heating needs. When the project is completed, Eos will be one of the largest wineries on California's Central Coast to run completely on alternative energy. Guided tours of the solar power system are available to visitors on request.

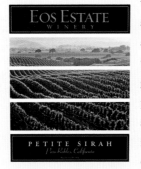

Hopmayer also aims to create world-class wines that harness the character of grapes from the estate and other regional vineyards. Hopmayer invested on extensive winery improvements, including a super-high-tech wine lab. He also replanted several vineyard blocks, added new vines, and recruited a new director of winemaking, Nathan Carlson. Hopmayer's commitment to sustainable agriculture and using only solar energy to provide energy needs lured green-minded Carlson to accept a position at Eos. A native of rural Minnesota and a key member of winemaking teams in Central California and Oregon's Dundee Hills, Carlson has more than a decade of winemaking experience and is known as an expert in regional climate and weather patterns. Carlson is spearheading the development of future releases from Eos estate holdings.

A cypress-lined drive leads up to the hospitality center, where visitors can taste their way through a complimentary flight of wines. An interactive self-guided tour of the winery facility explains the winemaking process—push a button at each station and a video presentation by the team members responsible for that particular area appears on forty-inch plasma screens. Eos encourages guests to sit outdoors amid the lush gardens, shaded by palm, olive, and oak trees, and enjoy the scenic views of the sun-splashed vineyards and rolling hills of this eco-friendly estate.

EOS ESTATE WINERY
5625 Hwy. 46 East
Paso Robles, CA 93446
805-239-2562
800-249-9463
info@eosvintage.com
www.eosvintage.com

OWNER: Jeff Hopmayer.

LOCATION: 6 miles east of U.S. 101.

APPELLATION: Paso Robles.

HOURS: 10 A.M.–5 P.M. daily (until 6 P.M. summer weekends).

TASTINGS: Complimentary. $10 for 5 reserve wines (includes wineglass).

TOURS: Self-guided during tasting room hours.

THE WINES: Cabernet Sauvignon, Chardonnay, Late Harvest Moscato, Malbec, Merlot, Muscat Canelli, Petite Sirah, Pinot Grigio, Sauvignon Blanc, Zinfandel, Zinfandel Port.

SPECIALTY: Block-designated Petite Sirah.

WINEMAKER: Nathan Carlson.

ANNUAL PRODUCTION: 125,000 cases.

OF SPECIAL NOTE: Fresh sandwiches, gourmet cheeses, and other picnic items available in tasting room. Picnic areas near rose garden overlooking vineyard. Limited reserve, special blends, and Cupa Grandis wines available only in tasting room.

NEARBY ATTRACTIONS: Barney Schwartz Park (lake, picnic areas); Estrella Warbird Museum (restored military aircraft, memorabilia).

HALTER RANCH VINEYARD

HALTER RANCH VINEYARD
8910 Adelaida Rd.
Paso Robles, CA 93446
805-226-9455
888-367-9977
www.halterranch.com

OWNER: Hansjörg Wyss.

LOCATION: 11 miles west of U.S. 101.

APPELLATION: Paso Robles.

HOURS: 11 A.M.–5 P.M. daily.

TASTINGS: $5 for 5–7 wines.

TOURS: By appointment.

THE WINES: Cabernet Sauvignon, Sauvignon Blanc, Syrah, Viognier.

SPECIALTIES: Ancestor (Estate Reserve, vintage blend of the best lots), El Pecado (port-style dessert wine), GSM (Grenache, Syrah, Mourvèdre blend).

WINEMAKER: Bill Sheffer.

ANNUAL PRODUCTION: 5,000 cases.

OF SPECIAL NOTE: Local olive oils and books on food and wine, as well as deli foods, available in tasting room. Picnic area located in garden outside tasting room. A registered champion coast live oak, one of the two largest specimens in the U.S., stands in the middle of one vineyard.

NEARBY ATTRACTION: Mt. Olive Organic Farm (tours, olive and olive oil tasting).

Since 1880, west side farmers have worked the soil of Halter Ranch Vineyard, leaving behind barns, bunkhouses, grain silos, and a glorious Victorian farmhouse as evidence of the site's long agricultural history. Turning up the driveway, lined with old oaks, cottage gardens, and a fifty-three-year-old orchard of olive and fruit trees, visitors find themselves transported to a scene of old California, where birdsong, whispering leaves, and a delicious calm prevail.

The carefully renovated farmhouse serves as the visual centerpiece of the ranch, whose owner, Swiss entrepreneur Hansjörg Wyss, believes in the preservation of historic structures. He not only restored a barn and recast the bunkhouse as restrooms sporting the original green doors, but also transformed the cabin-sized carriage house into an elegant tasting room fitted with broad windows and a curved, cherrywood tasting bar that glows in the natural light. Here, tasters can sip, swirl, and compare their impressions with winemaker tasting notes, or they can simply absorb the pastoral peace. If hunger strikes, a refrigerated case of cheeses, meats, and locally baked breads offers snacks for nibbling while lounging on the wide lawn or creekside patio.

Wyss, who bought the nine-hundred-acre ranch in 2000, expanded the original fifty-five-acre vineyard, planted by former owners in the late 1990s, to two hundred fifty acres. He tripled the number of varietals planted to nineteen and asked viticulturist Mitch Wyss (no relation) to create a vineyard that would last a hundred years or more. To ensure longevity of the vines, Mitch committed to a program of sustainable practices that includes the use of organic products and biodynamic preparations, as well as some dry farming. He maintains gardens for beneficial insects near the vines, refrains from spraying harsh chemicals, and relies on a tireless crew of chickens, what he calls his vineyard swat team, to eliminate destructive pests.

Mitch lives on the ranch with his wife, Leslie, who manages the office and tasting room, which opened in 2005. Winemaker Bill Sheffer joined the Halter Ranch team in 2006, bringing with him twenty years of experience, much of it with Paso Robles fruit. In the summer of 2008, Sheffer's fellow winemakers named him Winemaker of the Year at the San Luis Obispo Wine Industry Awards.

To honor the past, owner Hansjörg Wyss named his estate reserve program Ancestor, and for the winery, he chose Halter, his mother's maiden name. Both selections indicate that he intends the ranch, the vineyards, and the glorious Victorian farmhouse to be around for at least another century.

JACK CREEK CELLARS

Just inside the shady gate at Jack Creek Cellars, a mound of fieldstones riddled with marine fossils suggests the proximity of the Pacific Ocean. From seven miles away, breezes funneled through the Templeton Gap—outlined in the near distance by a chaparral-covered ridgeline bordering Highway 46 West—carry the damp scent of the seashore. The long driveway skirts a forty-acre vineyard and climbs a gentle slope past a bright red barn before turning in at the beige winery that doubles as a tasting room. To the south, a hilltop house rises from the center of the vineyard, affording owners Doug and Sabrina Kruse a clear view of the activity at the tidy facility.

The location may be off the beaten path, but Doug and Sabrina Kruse chose to have the tasting room on-site so visitors can get a firsthand look at winery operations, from pruning to hose wrangling to the excitement  of harvest. As tasting room manager, Sabrina appreciates the ease with which she can pop into the winery to greet her guests, as well as the opportunity to forge personal relationships with customers. Little more than a copper-topped bar in an airy corner, the tasting area has been carved from the workspace of the winery, putting visitors in the thick of things as Doug monitors tanks or racks wine just a few feet away. If time allows, the Kruses may even treat tasters to a quick winery tour or barrel samples of the latest vintage.

When Doug and Sabrina moved to the Central Coast and bought their seventy-five-acre property in 1997, they intended to plant a vineyard, grow their family, and farm their grapes for sale only. Two children and a few years later, an innocent foray into garage winemaking turned into a passionate pursuit that eventually led to the launch of the Jack Creek Cellars label. In 2002 the couple announced their first commercial vintage: a Syrah and a select bottling of the notoriously fickle Pinot Noir, which now reigns as their signature varietal.

Doug learned the vintner's craft from the ground up, through hands-on experience in both the winery and the vineyard, where he believes the real magic happens. He acknowledges the help he received from industry friends, who generously shared their knowledge and time, and confesses that he and Sabrina pursued their winery dream simply "for the love of it."

The Kruses, who admittedly favor wine over flash, plan to keep their family-run winery small so they can continue to do most of the work themselves. Together, they offer a quartet of estate-grown wines and a winery experience mere minutes from the beach.

JACK CREEK CELLARS
5265 Jack Creek Rd.
Templeton, CA 93465
805-226-8283
info@jackcreekcellars.com
www.jackcreekcellars.com

OWNERS: Doug and Sabrina Kruse.

LOCATION: 6.5 miles west of U.S. 101, just off Hwy. 46 West.

APPELLATION: Paso Robles.

HOURS: 11 A.M.–4:30 P.M. Friday–Sunday; weekdays by appointment, if available.

TASTINGS: $7 for 4 wines; $10 for 7 reserve wines (when available).

TOURS: By appointment or when time allows.

THE WINES: Chardonnay, Grenache, Pinot Noir, Syrah.

SPECIALTY: Estate Pinot Noir.

WINEMAKER: Doug Kruse.

ANNUAL PRODUCTION: 2,500 cases.

OF SPECIAL NOTE: Winery and tasting room are in center of vineyard. Library reserve wines available only in tasting room.

NEARBY ATTRACTION: Mt. Olive Organic Farm (tours, olive and olive oil tasting).

L'AVENTURE WINERY

L'AVENTURE WINERY
2815 Live Oak Rd.
Paso Robles, CA 93446
805-227-1588
tastingroom@
aventurewine.com
www.aventurewine.com

OWNER: Stephan Asséo.

LOCATION: 3 miles west of intersection of U.S. 101 and U.S. 46 West.

APPELLATION: Paso Robles.

HOURS: 11 A.M.–4 P.M. Thursday–Sunday.

TASTINGS: $10 for 4–6 wines.

TOURS: By appointment.

THE WINES: Cabernet Sauvignon, Estate Côte à Côte (Mourvèdre, Grenache, Syrah blend), Estate Cuvée (Syrah, Cabernet Sauvignon, Petit Verdot blend), Optimus (Cabernet Sauvignon, Syrah, Petit Verdot blend), Roussanne, Syrah.

SPECIALTIES: Premium Paso Robles blends.

WINEMAKER: Stephan Asséo.

ANNUAL PRODUCTION: 8,000 cases.

OF SPECIAL NOTE: Most wines available only in tasting room.

NEARBY ATTRACTION: Paso Robles City Park (site of festivals, summer concerts, farmers market).

A self-described purveyor of bottled pleasure, L'Aventure's Stephan Asséo cautions against overintellectualizing wine because, in his view, "you either like it or you don't." In 1996 the native Parisian decided to escape the French *appellation contrôllée* system, which regulates all aspects of winemaking to guarantee the quality of wines coming from key regions of France. Leaving a successful career in Bordeaux, he came to Paso Robles, where he could plant

the varietals of his choice and blend his wines as he pleased. Two years later, he spotted his future vineyard on 127 acres at the end of a dirt road in the heart of the Templeton Gap. Here, he divided 58 acres into thirty-nine blocks and planted 2,100 vines to the acre, tripling the average density of area vineyards to match the European model. Forced to compete for moisture and nutrients, the closely spaced vines produce a lighter crop than those with plenty of room, but their struggle infuses the resulting fruit with wonderfully concentrated varietal flavors.

Today, these vines greet visitors heading up the long unpaved driveway. Fronted by a lush lawn, the no-nonsense winery bears witness to Asséo's quest to make his estate-grown wines instinctively and unencumbered by arbitrary rules. The narrow tasting room set in a corner of the winery contains transparent cylinders displaying the region's fossil-rich soil, and a wall-mounted screen plays a slide show of vineyard scenes. Behind the wooden tasting bar, a window provides a serene view into the barrel room, leaving tasters free to concentrate on Asséo's complex, vineyard-driven wines.

Even after twenty-nine years in the wine industry, Asséo greets each harvest with excitement, hand-sorting his grapes and calculating their myriad variables. He revels in blending varietals and vineyard blocks to make wines representative of each vintage. Except for Roussanne, he focuses on luscious reds, selecting the final blends for his signature Optimus and Estate Cuvée a full ten months before bottling.

Born into a nonagricultural family, Asséo chose to become a farmer at age fourteen, when French schools require students to select a career path. Influenced by his wine-loving father, he opted for viticulture, "the most interesting branch of agriculture," and still considers himself more grower than winemaker. When Asséo moved his family to the west side of Paso Robles, his wife took over administrative tasks, while their children roamed the property. The epic adventure for which his winery was named has evolved beyond a simple search for creative freedom and into an haute couture estate, where Asséo can farm, live well, and blend freely.

LAETITIA VINEYARD & WINERY

The stunning views from the hilltop decks at Laetitia Vineyard & Winery rival the best on the Central Coast: a panorama of vineyards, the pastoral Arroyo Grande Valley, and the Pacific Ocean, just three miles to the west. In 1982 this gorgeous site captivated French viticulturists from Champagne Deutz, the esteemed Champagne house, who were searching for a suitable location to grow grapes and produce *méthode champenoise* sparkling wines in the United States. The viticulturalists were also impressed with the property's volcanic soils and climates, which resembled those in their native Epernay, France, and would promote high acid and minerality. They planted 185 acres to Pinot Noir, Chardonnay, and Pinot Blanc in specific sites chosen for their soil profile, exposure, and microclimate, and established Maison Deutz, a winery that quickly earned a reputation for outstanding sparkling wines.

In 1997 vineyard owner Jean-Claude Tardivat purchased Maison Deutz and renamed the winery Laetitia after his daughter. The winery's focus began to shift from sparkling wine to still wine production of Burgundian-style varietals, and experimentation revealed the vineyards' potential as a premier site for growing Pinot Noir. A year later, the winery was acquired by a partnership that included Selim Zilkha. In 2001 Zilkha obtained sole proprietorship of Laetitia.

Today the 1,800-acre Laetitia ranch includes 620 acres of vineyard blocks, with 430 acres devoted to Pinot Noir. Laetitia also owns a second vineyard, Santa Barbara Highlands, at a 3,200-foot elevation, sixty miles inland in the Cuyama Valley. This vineyard grows mostly Bordeaux varietals for Laetitia's Barnwood line of wines. The Hickey family manages nearly all day-to-day winery business. Winemaker Eric Hickey, who has worked at the winery since 1990, directs the still wine production and vineyard operations. Eric's father, Dave Hickey, began his career at Maison Deutz in 1985. He continues the winery's French tradition by making sparkling wines in the *champenoise* method, producing bubbles during a secondary fermentation in the bottle rather than in barrels. Eric's mother, Carmen, manages the tasting room, and his brother, Dustin, helps out in the cellar.

Visitors to the casual, country-style tasting room can view the adjacent press room, which houses two rare Coquard wooden basket presses, made in France, that Dave Hickey uses to press estate-grown Pinot Noir, Chardonnay, and Pinot Blanc grapes. These are the only such presses operated in the United States. Outdoors, visitors can relax in Adirondack chairs under yellow and white umbrellas on a lawn, above the gravity-flow winery and sweeping scenes of the ocean beyond.

LAETITIA VINEYARD & WINERY
453 Laetitia Vineyard Dr.
Arroyo Grande, CA 93420
805-474-7651
888-809-VINE
www.laetitiawine.com

OWNER: Selim Zilkha.

LOCATION: Directly off U.S. 101, between towns of Nipomo and Pismo Beach.

APPELLATION: Arroyo Grande Valley.

HOURS: 11 A.M.–5 P.M. daily.

TASTINGS: $10 for 5 wines; $10 for 5 reserve wines.

TOURS: None.

THE WINES: Brut Cuvée and Brut Rosé sparkling wines, Cabernet, Chardonnay, Pinot Noir, Syrah.

SPECIALTIES: Estate Pinot Noir, *méthode champenoise* sparkling wines.

WINEMAKERS: Eric Hickey (still wines); Dave Hickey (sparkling wines).

ANNUAL PRODUCTION: 30,000 cases.

OF SPECIAL NOTE: Visitors can see fully operational press room. Three picnic areas with umbrellas; bocce ball court on-site. Gift shop offering clothing, stemware, and books. Select Pinot Noirs and Barnwood wines from Santa Barbara Highlands vineyard available only in tasting room.

NEARBY ATTRACTIONS: Arroyo Grande Village (Old West downtown with historic walking tour); Pismo State Beach (swimming, hiking, camping).

LONE MADRONE

LONE MADRONE
2485 Hwy. 46 West
Paso Robles, CA 93446
805-238-0845
info@lonemadrone.com
www.lonemadrone.com

OWNERS: Neil Collins,
Jackie Meisinger.

LOCATION: 2.5 miles
from downtown Paso
Robles on Hwy. 46 West.

APPELLATIONS: Paso Robles,
York Mountain.

HOURS: 10:30 A.M.–5 P.M.
daily.

TASTINGS: $10 for 5 wines
(includes complimentary
wineglass).

TOURS: None.

THE WINES: Alvarinho, Bar-
bera, Cabernet Sauvignon,
Nebbiolo, Petite Sirah,
Picpoul Blanc, Roussanne,
Syrah, Tannat, Zinfandel.

SPECIALTIES: Rhône varietals,
west side Zinfandel blends,
hard apple cider.

WINEMAKER: Neil Collins.

ANNUAL PRODUCTION:
3,500 cases.

OF SPECIAL NOTE: Themed
herb gardens and shaded
lawn for picnics. On-site
nursery sells fresh and dried
herbs and 400 varieties of
potted plants. Events include
mid-August Basil Fest and
summer Sundays in the Garden. Local and international
artwork, glassware, and
jewelry for sale. Most wines
available only in tasting
room.

NEARBY ATTRACTIONS:
Templeton Park (events
including weekly summer
concerts); Jack Creek Farms
(demonstration gardens,
pick-your-own produce,
May–November).

Rising from the ashes of a 2004 fire that destroyed a once thriving herb farm, the Lone Madrone tasting room stands tall and inviting, a rough-hewn wooden barn set amid lawns and gardens laced with meandering trails. A wisteria-draped arbor ushers visitors onto the grounds, where a footpath curves past the surviving nursery and a Wonderland-worthy tree house before ending at the tall french doors of the tasting room. Inside, soft light reveals a lodgelike cedar-paneled interior stocked with artisan goods that include jewelry, ceramic ware, woven baskets, and packaged herbs. Signage tells a tale of philanthropy, for a percentage of the proceeds from many items supports communities in Africa, as well as local nonprofit organizations.

Owned by Neil Collins and  Jackie Meisinger, siblings who hail from England, Lone Madrone produces unusual offerings with names to match. From Barfandel (made with Barbera, Zinfandel, and Petite Sirah) to the unoaked Zin of Steel, the wines reflect a spirit of innovation and lighthearted fun.

Winemaker Neil Collins prac- tices what he calls a natural style of winemaking, using native and ambient yeasts, and resisting any urge to manipulate flavors. He welcomes the challenge of working with odd or difficult varietals, such as Tannat and Picpoul Blanc, and since he has no vineyards of his own, he maintains close relationships with west side Paso Robles growers who sustainably farm the kind of fruit he favors.

Trained as a French chef, Collins first came to Paso Robles in 1988 to visit Meisinger, who had moved to the area seven years earlier. He launched his viticultural career by working one crush at Wild Horse Winery and then apprenticing at Adelaida Cellars for five years, before becoming wine-maker at Tablas Creek Vineyard, where he continues in that role. In 1996 Collins purchased some York Mountain appellation Cabernet Sauvignon and made a little wine for himself, following up with a Nebbiolo. As Collins and Meisinger debated the merits of starting their own winery, a friend offered to invest, and Lone Madrone—named for a shade tree at the first vineyard that provided them with fruit—was born in 2003.

When Collins and Meisinger, who handles the business end of the winery, opened their tasting room in 2006, they were determined to return the grounds to their prefire glory. Now, a restored Victorian house anchors one corner of the property, while aromatic gardens offer a sheltered spot for savoring Lone Madrone's distinctive wines.

MALOY O'NEILL VINEYARDS

Affectionately known among friends and fellow winemakers as "the mad scientist," Shannon O'Neill crafts thirty-six different wines in lots as small as twenty-two cases. He admits that his penchant for variety poses marketing challenges, but delights that he can always pour something new for those who visit his Romanesque, stone-fronted tasting room near the eastern edge of the Paso Robles appellation.

O'Neill and his wife, Maureen, who lent her maiden name (Maloy) to the winery's shingle, make signature extracted wines famed for their varietal intensity, balancing the program with a handful of lighter offerings. The couple does everything by hand—from harvesting the fruit, to racking via gravity flow, to closing each bottle with a manual corker—because they believe the effort yields better wine. This hands-on approach extends to the tasting room, where the O'Neills often preside, pouring their wines amid the amber and ruby glow of stained glass windows set into Venetian plaster walls. Designed by Maureen, the spacious room evokes a vintage farmhouse stocked with fine wine, imported ceramics, and original art.

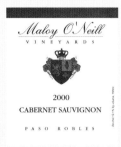

Under the tongue-in-cheek aegis of MOV-U (Maloy O'Neill Vineyard University), the couple offers lively seminars in wine pairing, wine evaluation, and even the finer points of deciphering a wine list. They hold their popular introduction to wine blending in the barrel room, where students create, cork, and capsule their own Bordeaux blend, producing a kind of liquid diploma to carry proudly home.

The O'Neill family first tackled viticulture in 1982, when Shannon's father converted a 180-acre barley field near Paso Robles into vineyards. Two years later, while at UC Davis, Shannon started making garage wine from the young Chardonnay vines, and when a sensory analysis course revealed the remarkable receptivity of his palate, he was officially deemed a "supertaster." Armed with a degree in fermentation science and enology, O'Neill navigated the corporate worlds of petroleum production and biotechnology until his marriage in 1993 led him to seek a more family-friendly lifestyle.

In 1998 he and Maureen chose a hilltop far from the Southern California beaches of his childhood and planted nearly a dozen varietals in an estate vineyard. A year later, they released their first commercial vintage. Maureen applied her years of experience working with software start-up companies to build a thriving business, while Shannon parlayed his scientific skills into a wildly eclectic lineup of wines. In 2005 the pair completed their elegant winery complex, where they welcome visitors, wine students, and the many neighbors who stop by just to see what's new on the tasting list.

MALOY O'NEILL VINEYARDS
5725 Union Rd.
Paso Robles, CA 93446
805-238-7320
winery@maloyoneill.com
www.maloyoneill.com

OWNERS: Shannon and Maureen O'Neill.

LOCATION: 3.9 miles east of Hwy. 46 East.

APPELLATION: Paso Robles.

HOURS: 10 A.M.–5 P.M. Thursday–Monday, except noon–5 p.m. Sunday; Tuesday and Wednesday by appointment.

TASTINGS: $5 for 8 wines (applicable to wine purchase). Reservations required for groups of 8 or more.

TOURS: By appointment.

THE WINES: Aglianico, Cabernet Franc, Cabernet Sauvignon, Chardonnay, Lagrein, Malbec, Malvasia Bianca, Merlot, Muscat Blanc, Petit Verdot, Petite Sirah, Pinot Grigio, Pinot Noir, Primitivo, Sangiovese, Sauvignon Blanc, Syrah, Tempranillo, Zinfandel.

SPECIALTIES: Red wine blends in small lots.

WINEMAKER: Shannon O'Neill.

ANNUAL PRODUCTION: 5,000 cases.

OF SPECIAL NOTE: Winery offers classes in wine tasting, wine-and-food pairings, blending, and other topics.

NEARBY ATTRACTIONS: Barney Schwartz Park (lake, picnic areas); Estrella Warbird Museum (restored military aircraft, memorabilia).

NADEAU FAMILY VINTNERS

NADEAU FAMILY VINTNERS
3860 Peachy Canyon Rd.
Paso Robles, CA 93446
805-239-3574
patrice@nadeaufamily
vintners.com
www.nadeaufamily
vintners.com

OWNERS: Robert and
Patrice Nadeau.

LOCATION: 4.5 miles west
of downtown Paso Robles.

APPELLATION: Paso Robles.

HOURS: 11 A.M.–5 P.M.
Friday–Sunday and most
holidays.

TASTINGS: Complimentary.

TOURS: Upon request
during business hours.

THE WINES: Grenache,
Petite Sirah, Roussanne,
Syrah, Tempranillo,
Viognier, Zinfandel.

SPECIALTIES: Rhône
varietals, Zinfandel.

WINEMAKER:
Robert Nadeau.

ANNUAL PRODUCTION:
2,000 cases.

OF SPECIAL NOTE: Tasting
room stocks custom-
made, wine-infused
chocolates. The Zinfandel
vineyard was propagated
from cuttings taken from
the historic Dusi Vineyard,
an 80-year-old planting
on the west side of Paso
Robles.

NEARBY ATTRACTION:
Paso Robles City Park
(site of festivals, summer
concerts, farmers market).

The drive to Nadeau Family Vintners winds past bicyclists, walnut orchards, and roads with names like Loose Horse Lane. At the winery's grape-colored sign, a turn through the white gate leads to the tasting room, a small, decked building bordered by a garden of head-pruned Petite Sirah vines. Near the door of the combination winery, laboratory, and tasting room—a structure that began life as a walnut barn—hangs a bell with a friendly sign inviting visitors who find the place locked to simply "ring bell for service."

Robert and Patrice Nadeau run what they call a micro-winery and take pride in doing everything themselves, from farming and harvesting the fruit to making, bottling, and selling the wine. The two touch every bottle, and since they also comprise the entire tasting room staff, visitors who drop in have the pleasure  of hearing wine stories told by the very people who lived them.

Beakers and test tubes sparkle behind the short tasting bar, hinting at the lab work that Robert, wine-maker and vineyard man-ager, does during off-hours. Patrice, a civil engineer when not tending to the winery's accounts and tasting room, admits that she often has to clean up the lab before she can greet customers. The tasting room boasts an unlikely collection of vintage wine bottles and oddities, such as a Geiger counter acquired after the Nadeaus released their first Critical Mass Zinfandel. Patrice explains that they wanted to make a big wine and chose the name "because nothing is bigger than critical mass." Soon after the wine's release, the custom-made chocolates in the tasting room were playfully renamed Ballistic Zin Bombs and Atomic Piles.

Robert, whose family moved to Paso Robles in the late 1970s, discovered the magic of wine in 1987, when he took a summer job at the Eberle Winery tasting room after serving in the U.S. Air Force. With Gary Eberle's help, he parlayed his chemistry background into a winemaking career that led him to work for a number of local producers until 1997, when the Nadeaus released their first wine. With about seven acres of vineyard at nearly two thousand feet in elevation, the Nadeaus grow mostly Zinfandel, with a little Grenache and Petite Sirah for variety. They buy fruit to supplement their small lots of mountain-grown reds, and each year source an unusual varietal, such as Tempranillo or Roussanne. Celebrating ten years in business, the two still favor big, lush reds and take special delight when customers taste through their wines, nod with approval, and then flash a happy, purple smile.

Opolo Vineyards

Heading through the gate at Opolo Vineyards, visitors enter a viticultural wonderland anchored by an unassuming tasting room: a converted tractor barn decorated to inspire guests to relax and have fun. Famed for its loyal fans and weekend festivities, often featuring grilled delicacies—from sausage and lamb to Cevapcici, a Serbian-style roll of minced beef—this event-driven destination serves up a lively mix of food, wine, and convivial pleasure. Guests can sip wine on the covered deck while taking in the vineyard views, or they can step inside, where giant posters brighten the walls and stacked barrels share space with cases of wine. At wooden planks laid atop oak barrels, friendly staffers pour the listed wines, and then, based on each taster's preferences, suggest others from the winery's thirty-some offerings.

Opolo Vineyards owners, Rick Quinn and David Nichols, share the winemaking duties and welcome feedback from the staff, information that they feel helps them produce wines with the widest customer appeal. When evaluating potential blends, they sometimes even ask tasting room visitors to weigh in on the decision.

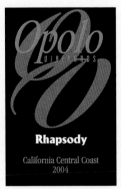

Rhapsody

California Central Coast
2004

A software developer and owner of a real estate brokerage, Quinn first made wine with his family in Minnesota. He revived the tradition when he moved to Southern California, where his successes inspired Nichols, his neighbor and the proprietor of a wireless electronics firm, to take up the hobby. In 1995, when Quinn's Merlot source dried up, the dynamic businessman planted his own vineyard on the west side of Paso Robles with an eye toward supplying his home winemaking needs and selling the rest of the crop to commercial producers. Two years later, Nichols bought the vineyard next to Quinn's and the two plunged into the grape-growing business, selling their fruit to such respected Napa Valley cellars as Niebaum-Coppola, St. Supéry, Fetzer, and Hess Collection. Today they farm three hundred acres of vineyards on the west and east side and continue to sell fruit to some of the finest wineries in the state.

In 1998 the partners noted an industry-wide surplus of grapes and began making wine under their own label in a bid to showcase their vineyards' quality and enhance grape sales. The partners bottled some Merlot, labeling half "Merlot" and the other half "Opolo," the name of a Dalmatian Coast wine selected to honor Quinn's heritage. Believing the wines to be different, friends overwhelmingly preferred the latter, making Opolo, in Nichols's words, the "slam dunk" choice for the name of their new enterprise. Ten years and thousands of cases later, the partners have created a viticultural destination with a well-earned reputation for treating visitors to a good time.

Opolo Vineyards
7110 Vineyard Dr.
Paso Robles, CA 93446
805-238-9593
sales@opolo.com
www.opolo.com

Owners: Rick Quinn, David Nichols.

Location: 8 miles west of U.S. 101.

Appellation: Paso Robles.

Hours: 10 a.m.–5 p.m. daily.

Tastings: Complimentary.

Tours: By appointment.

The Wines: Cabernet Franc, Cabernet Sauvignon, Chardonnay, Grenache, Malbec, Merlot, Mourvèdre, Muscat Canelli, Petit Verdot, Petite Sirah, Pinot Grigio, Pinot Noir, Roussanne, Sangiovese, Syrah, Tempranillo, Viognier, Zinfandel.

Specialties: Montagna-Mare (Barbera, Sangiovese blend), Mountain Zinfandel, Rhapsody (Cabernet Franc, Merlot, Cabernet Sauvignon, Petit Verdot blend).

Winemakers: Rick Quinn, David Nichols.

Annual Production: 40,000 cases.

Of Special Note: On-site bed-and-breakfast, The Inn at Opolo. Cooking classes and Chef's Table wine-and-food pairings by appointment. Harvest grape stomp and various weekend events.

Nearby Attraction: Mt. Olive Organic Farm (tours, olive and olive oil tasting).

ORCHID HILL VINEYARD

ORCHID HILL VINEYARD
1140 Pine St.
Paso Robles, CA 93446
805-237-7525
info@orchidhillwine.com
www.orchidhillwine.com

OWNER:
Mike Schenkhuizen.

LOCATION: Downtown
Paso Robles.

APPELLATION: Paso Robles.

HOURS: Noon–6 P.M. daily,
or by appointment.

TASTINGS: $5 for 5 wines;
$10 for 7 reserve wines
(applicable to purchase).

TOURS: None.

THE WINES: Grenache,
Muscat Canelli, Pinot
Grigio, Pinot Noir,
Sangiovese, Syrah,
Viognier, Zinfandel.

SPECIALTIES: Pinot Noir,
Syrah, Zinfandel.

WINEMAKER: Dan Kleck.

ANNUAL PRODUCTION:
3,500 cases.

OF SPECIAL NOTE: Private
wine-and-cheese pairings
by appointment. Original
art sold in tasting room.

NEARBY ATTRACTION:
Paso Robles City Park
(site of festivals, summer
concerts, farmers market).

hen visitors push through the door at the Orchid Hill Vineyard tasting room in downtown Paso Robles, color greets the eye as primary hues dance on framed paintings and pastels glow from a dozen live orchids. Creative lighting showcases the handcrafted cabinetry and stamped concrete floor. Essentially an art gallery with a built-in tasting bar, the long, airy space culminates in the Orchid Room, an elegant retreat where tasters can enjoy private wine-and-cheese pairings amid even more exotic orchids.

Orchid Hill Vineyard is owned by Mike and Estrella Schenkhuizen, who named their winery in honor of Estrella's passion for growing the flowering beauties. When one orchid begins to fade, she takes it back into her hothouse at home and replaces it with a fresh specimen, sharing her expertise by creating a rare treat for all who enter the tasting room. When not working with her prize plants, she creates the colorful jewelry displayed behind the counter.

Mike, who has always enjoyed fine wines, found a way to expand his involvement with the vintner's craft when he and Estrella moved to the Central Coast in 1998. The couple bought fifty-one acres in the Templeton Gap region of west Paso Robles—where evening breezes quickly cool the sun-drenched land—and planted about half of the property to grapes. The steeply sloping hills are covered with shale and limestone soils that support both Zinfandel and Pinot Noir vines, as well as several Rhône varietals, and produce small berries loaded with color and intense flavors.

For two years, Mike sold all of his fruit to local wineries, but when prices softened in 2001, he decided to launch his own label. He hired veteran winemaker Dan Kleck, a consultant with more than two decades of experience, to bring out Orchid Hill Vineyard's first release in 2002. Kleck continues to make the wine at Paso Robles Wine Services, a fully equipped facility that caters to small producers, while Mike, who divides his time between Paso Robles and the Bay Area, stays involved by tasting through the barrels regularly and joining Kleck in brainstorming sessions over blending and stylistic direction. With the opening of the tasting room in 2007, Mike can share his love of wine with his customers, and Estrella has the perfect place to showcase her ever-changing collection of exquisite orchids.

Ortman Family Vineyards

Among the newest tasting rooms in downtown Paso Robles, Ortman Family Vineyards opened in 2008, seven years after the winery's founding by one of the region's esteemed old winemaking families. The brainchild of two generations of Ortmans, the enterprise marks a return to the family's artisan winery roots and a passing of the winemaking torch to Chuck Ortman's son, Matt.

Boasting more than four decades of combined industry experience, the Ortmans launched the tasting room as a new home for the "Ortman style," a winemaking approach that values the character of the grape above all—a notion considered wildly innovative when Chuck Ortman introduced it to the region twenty-five years ago. As wine master, he continues to promote the blending of different vineyards to craft more complex wines, as well as the judicious use of oak. Matt, who handles daily cellar operations, is refining the family's famous style to include vintages with enhanced intensity and power. Adding her deft touch to the family business, Lisa, Matt's wife, sees to marketing tasks, tasting room duties, and "whatever else needs to be done."

The storefront tasting room offers a quiet spot to evaluate the wines, made from fruit grown in Paso Robles, Edna Valley, Santa Rita Hills, Napa Valley, and Oregon. It is also an ideal starting point from which to explore downtown shops on foot. A haven of natural fibers and earth tones, the tasting room is a study in green building materials, including a cork floor, sorghum-based paneling, and tiles made from recycled glass, all a reflection of the Ortmans' progressive spirit.

Chuck Ortman soundly demonstrated that spirit in 1968, when a friend inspired him to trade a career in graphic arts for an entry-level position at Heitz Wine Cellars in Napa Valley. He learned to make wine under Joe Heitz; became a consultant to acclaimed producers such as Far Niente, Shafer, and St. Clement; and pioneered the barrel fermentation of California Chardonnay while working at Spring Mountain Vineyard in 1973. Six years later, he started the Charles Ortman label—later renamed Meridian—with Chardonnay grapes from Edna Valley. Meridian was subsequently acquired by Beringer and moved to Paso Robles in the late 1980s, with Chuck staying on as winemaker. The success of Meridian Vineyards helped put Paso Robles on the map at a time when the area had just a few dozen wineries. Matt Ortman, who grew up helping his father during harvests in Napa Valley, earned a degree and experience in construction engineering before turning to winemaking. When Chuck was wrapping up his time at Meridian, Matt decided to help the family return to its artisan winemaking roots and ultimately to dedicate himself to advancing the inimitable Ortman style.

Ortman Family Vineyards
1317 Park St.
Paso Robles, CA 93446
805-237-9009
info@ortmanvineyards.com
www.ortmanvineyards.com

Owners: Ortman family.

Location: Downtown Paso Robles.

Appellation: Paso Robles.

Hours: Noon–6 P.M. (5 P.M. in winter) Sunday–Thursday; noon–7 P.M. Friday and Saturday.

Tastings: $6 for 5–7 wines (applicable to purchase).

Tours: None.

The Wines: Cabernet Sauvignon, Chardonnay, Petite Sirah, Pinot Noir, Sangiovese, Syrah.

Specialties: Chardonnay, Cuvée Eddy (Syrah, Grenache, Mourvèdre blend), Pinot Noir.

Winemakers: Chuck Ortman, Matt Ortman.

Annual Production: 6,000 cases.

Of Special Note: Certain limited-edition wines available only in tasting room.

Nearby Attraction: Paso Robles City Park (site of festivals, summer concerts, farmers market).

PEACHY CANYON WINERY

PEACHY CANYON WINERY
1480 N. Bethel Rd.
Templeton, CA 93465
805-239-1918
866-335-1918
tastingroom@
peachycanyon.com
www.peachycanyon.com

OWNERS: Doug and
Nancy Beckett.

LOCATION: 1.5 miles west
of U.S. 101.

APPELLATION: Paso Robles.

HOURS: 11 A.M.–5 P.M. daily.

TASTINGS: $5 for 6 wines
(applicable to purchase).

TOURS: None.

THE WINES: Cabernet
Franc, Cabernet Sauvi-
gnon, Merlot, Petite Sirah,
Viognier, Zinfandel.

SPECIALTY: Zinfandel.

WINEMAKER: Josh Beckett.

ANNUAL PRODUCTION:
80,000 cases.

OF SPECIAL NOTE:
Locally made condiments,
home accessories, and gift
items sold in tasting room.
Picnic area overlooking
vineyard. Events include
Zinfandel Weekend
(March), Winefest (May),
Westfest (September), and
Harvest Weekend (Octo-
ber). Port VI available in
tasting room only.

NEARBY ATTRACTIONS:
Templeton Park (events
including weekly summer
concerts); Jack Creek
Farms (demonstration
gardens, pick-your-own
produce, May–November).

A crown jewel among the historic tasting rooms of Paso Robles, the hospitality headquarters of Peachy Canyon Winery once served as the Bethel Road School House. Since 1886, the white clapboard building has stood on the site. It is now carpeted with lawn and twisted oak trees, and its academic origins nicely mirror the careers of owners Doug and Nancy Beckett, who worked as schoolteachers before entering the wine business. The grounds of what is now known as the Old School House tasting room offer welcome shade and a classic gazebo for relaxing on a warm day, and a latticed deck for cooler weather. Nearby, Doug's first basket press, used to make Peachy Canyon's debut wine in 1988, poses as both garden art and a reminder of humble beginnings.

Shortly after the Becketts moved to Paso Robles in 1982 to raise their children in a rural environment, Doug joined the ranks of home winemakers by crafting Zinfandel in five-gallon water bottles. He used a pitchfork to scoop grapes into a portable crusher and borrowed barrels from a friend. When the harvest ended, Doug was certain that winemaking was his calling.

After twenty years in business, the winery has grown from five hundred to eighty thousand cases produced annually, and the Beckett family farms a hundred acres of their own fruit, as well as purchases grapes from nearly two dozen local growers. The couple's older son, Josh, has worked at the winery for a decade and been the winemaker of record since 2003. His younger brother, Jake, apprenticed as vineyard manager for several years before hitting the road as general sales manager in 2005.

Famed for their Zinfandels, Peachy Canyon Winery produces more than fifteen other hand-crafted small-batch varietals and blends. Among them is only one white wine: Viognier. Visitors to the tasting room can enjoy the wines while browsing a gift shop filled with locally made condiments, books, and an array of other items. During the colder months, flames crackle in the fireplace.

The Becketts once lived in the two-story Peachy Canyon Road house pictured on the wine label, and they wanted to reinforce the regional identity by choosing a familiar reference point, but the story of the name goes a little deeper into local color. According to reliable lore, an old horse thief whose surname was Peachy used to hide out with his four-legged booty in caves concealed amid the rugged outcroppings of the west side. The last member of the Peachy family, a dentist, left the area years ago, but the legend and the distinctive name live on.

PENMAN SPRINGS VINEYARD

Skirted by oak savannas and tide-sculpted hills, Penman Springs Vineyard perches atop a broad rise just three miles east of downtown Paso Robles, though the rural landscape suggests a more remote location. Beyond the short driveway, a white board-and-batten tasting room invites visitors to push open the glass door and step into what owners Carl and Beth McCasland laughingly refer to as "grandma's house."

Inside, Beth and her able assistant, Rosie Sacasa, call cheerful hellos, as tasters decide whether to work the jigsaw puzzle (a tradition Beth started just after the tasting room opened in 2000), browse the Penman Pantry selection of locally made condiments, or sample the handcrafted wine made from estate fruit. Occasionally pairing cheeses, Beth aims to make tastings of all, enjoyable. The McCaslands art and wine, and as Beth pours, The art is on the bottle as well as Furbacher, created the image used color wheel comprised of angular

the wines with artisan breads and relaxed, educational, and, most treasure the relationship between she urges visitors to "taste the art!" inside it: Beth's brother, Richard on the winery's logo of a distinctive pieces of stained glass.

While Beth trades quips with customers, Carl, the serious viti-culturist, is usually out making the rounds in his vineyard. The McCaslands bought what Carl calls their "garden" in 1996, after selling Sun King Container, a plant they owned in Texas. Their purchase included a forty-acre parcel with twenty-eight acres of established grapevines. Carl removed more than half of the original vineyard and then developed the entire forty acres, following sustainable agricultural principles. He uses a variety of trellis systems, always focusing on the techniques for managing the grapevine canopies that allow sunshine and warm air to ripen his grapes to perfection. Inspiration for this approach came from Dr. Richard Smart's seminal book, *Sunlight into Wine*.

Two years after the McCaslands acquired the property, they launched the Penman Springs label. That same year, Larry Roberts came on board as winemaker, a welcome addition to the team and a craftsman who has proven to be especially gifted in the intricate mysteries of fermentation. Roberts also serves as a sounding board for Carl, who reads constantly to refine his practices and enjoys discussing the finer points of viniculture. He and Carl initially crushed a Merlot and Cabernet Sauvignon behind the soon-to-be tasting room and followed up with small lots of Chardonnay and Muscat Blanc. Five years later, as annual production topped a thousand cases, the McCaslands moved their winery operation to Paso Robles Wine Services, where they will remain until their on-site winery is built. Meanwhile, they continue to welcome visitors to their east side perch.

PENMAN SPRINGS VINEYARD
1985 Penman Springs Rd.
Paso Robles, CA 93446
805-237-7959
inquiry@penmansprings.
com
www.penmansprings.com

OWNERS: Carl and
Beth McCasland.

LOCATION: 2.5 miles east
of Hwy. 46 East.

APPELLATION: Paso Robles.

HOURS: 11 A.M.–5 P.M.
Thursday–Sunday.
Closed January.

TASTINGS: $5 (applicable
to wine purchase).

TOURS: None.

THE WINES: Cabernet
Sauvignon, Merlot, Muscat
Blanc, Petite Sirah, Syrah.

SPECIALTIES: Cabernet
Sauvignon, Estate Old
Block, Meritage Estate
Artisan Cuvée.

WINEMAKER:
Larry Roberts.

ANNUAL PRODUCTION:
2,400 cases.

OF SPECIAL NOTE: Penman
Pantry stocks books, local
condiments, one-of-a-kind
jewelry, and handmade
goat milk soap. Late-
harvest and fortified
wines available only at
tasting room.

NEARBY ATTRACTIONS:
Barney Schwartz Park
(lake, picnic areas);
Estrella Warbird Museum
(restored military aircraft,
memorabilia).

PIANETTA WINERY

PIANETTA WINERY
829 13th St.
Paso Robles, CA 93446
805-226-4005
info@pianettawinery.com
www.pianettawinery.com

OWNERS: Pianetta family.

LOCATION: Downtown
Paso Robles.

APPELLATION: Monterey,
Paso Robles.

HOURS: Noon–6 P.M. Sunday, Monday, Wednesday,
and Thursday; 11 A.M.–
7 P.M. Friday and Saturday.

TASTINGS: $5 for 6 wines.

TOURS: None.

THE WINES: Cabernet
Sauvignon, Petite Syrah,
Sangiovese, Shiraz, Syrah,
Zinfandel.

SPECIALTIES: Bilancio (Cabernet Sauvignon, Syrah
blend), Tuscan Nights
(Cabernet Sauvignon,
Sangiovese, Petite Syrah
blend).

WINEMAKER: John Pianetta.

ANNUAL PRODUCTION:
2,500 cases.

OF SPECIAL NOTE: Barrel
tastings at the winery
(14 miles north of tasting
room) by appointment.
Wines available only
online and in the tasting
room.

NEARBY ATTRACTION:
Paso Robles City Park
(site of festivals, summer
concerts, farmers market).

For four generations, the Pianetta family has farmed in California, first growing produce in the Bay Area and shipping it worldwide from the early 1920s through the 1970s, and later managing a vineyard in Lodi. In 1996, on the heels of a career as an airline pilot, John Pianetta plunged back into the family business by purchasing ninety-five acres about a dozen miles north of Paso Robles and planting sixty-seven acres of red wine grapes. Impressed by the high quality of this Monterey County fruit, Pianetta's buyers encouraged him to make a little wine to build an identity for his vineyard. Remembering the fun he had as a child helping his grandfather craft Zinfandel into homemade wine, he followed up on the suggestion.

John's daughter, Caitlin, who has driven a tractor since she could reach the pedals, gladly joined the effort, helping with crush,  chemical analysis, and marketing, beginning with their very first vintage in 2002. At Caitlin's suggestion that they sell directly to customers, the family opened a tasting room in 2006 and became among the first area wineries to hang a shingle in downtown Paso Robles. As befitting a venerable farming family, the Pianettas chose one of the city's oldest structures for their tasting room: the Grangers Union Building, dating from 1886 and once a showroom for everything from tinware to buggies. To create the feel of a ranch house, they installed wooden arbors against the walls and hung photographs of farm scenes taken from the family album. In the storefront window rests a wonderfully appropriate keepsake: the very pump that Grandpa Pianetta used to move his homemade wine from barrel to barrel.

Spacious and inviting, the tasting room features hardwood floors, a four-sided, granite-topped tasting bar, and bouquets of fresh flowers. Wine rules here, so there is little in the way of logo wear and gift items. In a spirit of lighthearted fun, Caitlin notes the first things tasters say when they sample the exclusively red lineup and jots them down on a nearby chalkboard. She believes that posting these spontaneous descriptors, such as "skirt flipper" and "Caitalicious Cab," helps to set a playful mood and put tasters at ease.

With Caitlin's two brothers serving in the U.S. Navy, father and daughter run the family wine business together. John handles the farming and winemaking, Caitlin manages the tasting room and marketing, and, when necessary, both willingly deploy tractors, pitchforks, and basket presses, working the land and reaping its bounty, just as generations of Pianettas before them have done.

RED SOLES WINERY

Aside from farming grapes and making estate wines, Red Soles Winery owner Randy Phillips laughingly admits that "everything is about feet," a declaration supported by his logo bearing scarlet footprints, and wine names ranging from Stiletto to Flip-Flop. The theme emerged in the early 2000s, after Randy and his wife, Cheryl, stomped red grapes, stepped on a white towel, and envisioned a label with her high-arched print on the right, his flatter one opposite.

Randy and Cheryl Phillips began growing grapes for sale in 1991 and today farm two hundred acres divided between the east and west sides of Paso Robles. They dubbed their vineyards Loverboy, after their grown son's amorous tendencies as a teen; Morning Glory, because Cheryl is a morning person; and Miracle's son, born nineteen years after two thousand tons of grapes to vintners all over California. their own label and debuted 2004. The two do most of the with Cheryl checking the grapes and Randy directing the vine-

Ranch, to honor their second their first. The couple harvests annually and sells their fruit They crush about 1 percent for their first wine, Kick-Off, in winery-related work themselves, as they come in during harvest yard crews. On weekends, both can be found pouring samples at the red-tile-roofed tasting room that they opened in 2007.

With advice from his consultant, Signe Zoller—whom Randy calls the "grande dame of California winemakers"—Randy crafts his wines in and around the tasting room, a converted equipment shed fitted with glass doors on two sides to allow a clear view of the action. When grapes come in, the press hums at the side door, fermentors bubble in the storage area, and later, bottling takes place near the driveway. Inside the tasting room, an elegant horseshoe-shaped bar of polished wood commands center stage. Colorful cloth chevrons hang from the high ceiling, and framed T-shirts documenting wine festivals and Randy's musical moods make up a veritable time line of the winery's history. Out back, tasters find tables and a patch of lawn where they can unpack a picnic lunch and relax over a bottle of wine.

Randy and Cheryl Phillips moved to the Paso Robles area from Orange County in Southern California in 1987, just as Randy was winding down his manifold career as a National Security Agency operative, high-tech inventor, and entrepreneur. Both had traveled here as children—Cheryl with her parents and Randy to visit his grandparents, who mined mercury near Adelaida—so they knew the region well. After thirty-eight years of marriage, Randy calls Cheryl "Big Boss," and in turn, she graciously accepts the winery truck's license plate spelling out Randy's favorite identity: Old Wino.

RED SOLES WINERY
3230 Oakdale Rd.
Paso Robles, CA 93446
805-226-9898
info@redsoleswinery.com
www.redsoleswinery.com

OWNERS: Randy and Cheryl Phillips.

LOCATION: 3 miles west of U.S. 101.

APPELLATION: Paso Robles.

HOURS: 11 A.M.–5:30 P.M. Monday–Saturday; noon–5 P.M. Sunday.

TASTINGS: $5 for 6 wines.

TOURS: None.

THE WINES: Cabernet Franc, Cabernet Sauvignon, Chardonnay, Petite Sirah, Syrah, Viognier, Zinfandel.

SPECIALTIES: Blue Suede (late harvest Syrah), Flip-Flop (Chardonnay, Viognier blend), Kick-Off (Petite Sirah, Zinfandel, Cabernet Sauvignon blend), Stiletto (late harvest Viognier).

WINEMAKER: Randy Phillips.

ANNUAL PRODUCTION: 2,000 cases.

OF SPECIAL NOTE: Picnic area available outside tasting room. Wines are available only online or in the tasting room.

NEARBY ATTRACTIONS: Templeton Park (events including weekly summer concerts); Jack Creek Farms (demonstration gardens, pick-your-own produce, May–November).

STACKED STONE CELLARS

STACKED STONE CELLARS
1525 Peachy Canyon Rd.
Paso Robles, CA 93446
805-238-7872
donald@stackedstone.com
www.stackedstone.com

OWNER: Donald Thiessen.

LOCATION: 1.5 miles west
of Spring St.

APPELLATION: Paso Robles.

HOURS: 11 A.M.–5 P.M.
Friday and Saturday;
noon–5 P.M. Sunday; week-
days by appointment.

TASTINGS: Complimentary
for 6 wines.

TOURS: By appointment.

THE WINES: Bordeaux,
Rhône, rosé blends.

SPECIALTIES: Estate
Zinfandel, Zin Stone.

WINEMAKER:
Donald Thiessen.

ANNUAL PRODUCTION:
2,000 cases.

OF SPECIAL NOTE: In summer, winery hosts concerts,
barbecues, and songwriters
open mic nights. Reserve
wines available only in
tasting room.

NEARBY ATTRACTION:
Paso Robles City Park
(site of festivals, summer
concerts, farmers market).

With its cottage gardens, canopy of oak trees, and weathered wooden buildings tucked into a shady hollow, Stacked Stone Cellars puts an old-world spin on the modern winery. Named for an ancient masonry technique, this small, self-contained facility features borders of fitted rocks culled from the vineyard, a grassy glen for picnicking, and a combined tasting bar, barrel room, and analysis lab that owner Donald Thiessen calls "the real deal." So real, in fact, that the person pouring behind the makeshift bar is usually Thiessen himself, a gregarious entrepreneur who loves people, wine, and swapping stories. He readily offers barrel samples and sometimes even creates blends right in the glass, encouraging tasters to learn about varietal flavors and trust their own palates.

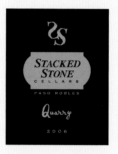

Thiessen, who grew up on an avocado ranch in Ventura, south of Santa Barbara, always dreamed of making a living from his own piece of land. First, though, he carved a colorful career path as a baker, beekeeper, chef, hunting guide, and hard-rock miner; produced educational films with television's Mr. Wizard; and founded a custom woodworking business that he continues to head.

Shortly after a 1976 vacation at nearby Lake Nacimiento that led him to explore the Paso Robles area, Thiessen bought his future vineyard. The land boasted little more than a prime location and barbed wire fence, but with characteristic gusto, he set about creating his own "paradise" by planting trees, laying out gardens, and building a home. In 1998 Thiessen terraced a south-facing slope for his dry-farmed, head-pruned vineyard, a task he describes as life threatening because of the treacherous incline and an underground nest of angry wasps stirred up by the bulldozer. He propagated and planted cuttings from his favorite local Zinfandel vines, and after trading the odd custom door or remodeling job for winemaking consultations, he released his first commercial vintage in 2002.

In 2008, after working solo for six years, Thiessen hired enologist Shawna Madigan to help him turn his fruit—70 percent estate and 30 percent purchased from local vineyards—into nuanced wines with just a touch of oak. He chose names with geologic imagery, such as Gem, Quarry, Zin Stone, and Rosetta, to highlight his notion that as a winemaker he essentially mines minerals from the limestone soil via the grapes and puts them into bottles.

A visit to Stacked Stone Cellars usually begins when Buck and Bailey, two amiable golden retrievers shaved to resemble lions, greet arriving guests and lead them to the tasting room. As pigeons coo from their nearby aviary and a splashing fountain whispers from a hillside, Donald Thiessen uncorks a fresh bottle of wine, happy to make new friends and share his little piece of paradise.

STILL WATERS VINEYARDS

At the end of a long lane, Still Waters Vineyards opens like an oasis amid the arid hills east of Templeton. Sixty acres of grapevines nearly encircle the winery, and as visitors wait for the automatic gate to swing open, herbal scents drift from the gardens ahead. Inside the deer fence, flowers tumble from half barrels, shrubs bloom alongside ancient oaks, and a green lawn begs for bare feet. Amid a fringe of tall grasses sparkles a koi pond festooned with lily pads and aerated by a series of cascading fountains crafted from surplus barrels

Owners Paul and Patty Hoover, who met while waterskiing on the "still waters" of a glassy lake, have created a landscape reminiscent of an outdoor restaurant, where guests can relax, share a picnic in the shade of a century-old olive grove, and soak up the serenity of a small family farm. The Hoovers hope that their guests will connect with the land that produces the winery's estate grapes and olive oil, and as agricultural ambassadors, they even give away produce from their half-acre garden in what Paul laughingly calls a "reverse farmers market." From a gentle rise, the tasting room invites visitors to amble across a shaded porch and into what feels like a country home furnished with a sofa, a fireplace, and copper kitchen fixtures. Here, Patty can often be found pouring samples, while Paul handles chores in the cellar.

In college, Paul studied agricultural business, made a little beer, and tended bar at a local resort, a job that exposed him to some of the world's finest wines. He forged a career in hotel and restaurant management, and later he became an insurance executive, a position he still holds. Paul and Patty married nearly thirty years ago. After making goat milk cheese with their 4-H-age children, they ventured into home winemaking, a hobby gone wild that led to the planting of a one-acre vineyard at their Atascadero home in 1995.

Eight years later, the couple got serious about expanding production, so they officially launched their winery and bought a vineyard that had been planted to Merlot and Cabernet Sauvignon ten years earlier. They grafted several acres of vines to increase variety, planted fourteen more acres next door, and began selling about 80 percent of their crop to eight other California wineries. Having struggled to find quality grapes as amateur vintners, the Hoovers gladly supply more than twenty home winemakers with fruit, advice, and expert consultation services. Although they have joined the ranks of professional winemakers, the Hoovers continue to live by their long-held credo: "Be small, have fun, and focus on quality."

STILL WATERS VINEYARDS
2750 Old Grove Ln.
Paso Robles, CA 93446
805-237-9231
winery@stillwatersvineyards.com
www.stillwatersvineyards.com

OWNERS: Paul and Patty Hoover.

LOCATION: 1.5 miles east of intersection of Creston Rd. and S. El Pomar Rd.

APPELLATION: Paso Robles.

HOURS: 11 A.M.–5 P.M. Thursday–Monday.

TASTINGS: $5 for 5 wines (applicable to purchase).

TOURS: Vineyard and winery tours by appointment. Self-guided Sustainable Growing Practices tour.

THE WINES: Cabernet Franc, Cabernet Sauvignon, Chardonnay, Malbec, Merlot, Pinot Gris, Sauvignon Blanc, Syrah, Syrah Rosé, Viognier, Zinfandel.

SPECIALTY: Reflections (Cabernet Sauvignon, Cabernet Franc, Malbec, Merlot, Syrah blend).

WINEMAKER: Paul Hoover.

ANNUAL PRODUCTION: 3,000 cases.

OF SPECIAL NOTE: Oil from 100-year-old estate olive trees offered for sampling and purchase in the tasting room. Wines available only in the tasting room. Food-and-wine pairings by appointment (fees vary).

NEARBY ATTRACTIONS: Barney Schwartz Park (lake, picnic areas); Estrella Warbird Museum (restored military aircraft, memorabilia).

SUMMERWOOD WINERY

SUMMERWOOD WINERY
2175 Arbor Rd.
Paso Robles, CA 93446
805-227-1365
info@summerwoodwine.
com
www.summerwoodwine.
com

OWNERS: Fukae family.

LOCATION: 1 mile west of
U.S. 101.

APPELLATION: Paso Robles.

HOURS: 10 A.M.–6 P.M. daily.

TASTINGS: $5 for 5 wines;
$10 for 5 reserve wines.

TOURS: By appointment.

THE WINES: Cabernet
Sauvignon, Chardonnay,
Roussanne, Syrah, Viognier.

SPECIALTIES: Diosa (Syrah,
Grenache, Mourvèdre
blend), Sentio (Cabernet
Sauvignon, Malbec, Petit
Verdot, Cabernet Franc,
Merlot blend).

WINEMAKER: Chris Cameron.

ANNUAL PRODUCTION:
4,800 cases.

OF SPECIAL NOTE: Grassy
picnic area. Saturday
afternoon food-and-wine
pairings (reservations required). Special events such
as concerts, workshops,
and winemaker dinners
held monthly. Croquet and
Viognier tournament in
July. On the winery
grounds is a nine-room
inn that serves gourmet
cuisine. Tasting room
boutique features wine
accessories, light snacks,
books, and gift items.
Wines available online and
in tasting room only.

NEARBY ATTRACTIONS:
Templeton Park (events
including weekly summer
concerts); Jack Creek
Farms (demonstration
gardens, pick-your-own
produce, May–November).

Framed by hedges, flowering shrubs, and majestic blue oaks, Summerwood Winery resembles a lavish country estate from a seemingly bygone era of ice-cream socials and leisurely croquet matches. Vineyards lap at the perimeter of snow-white structures skirted with inviting porches, and a pergola draped with edible grapes links a gazebo-like room on the lawn to the well-appointed tasting complex. A combination lobby, gift shop, and wine center, the winery's tasting room boasts an exposed beam ceiling and elegant slate floor inlaid with African mahogany. Plush seating and a fireplace for winter warmth offer creature comforts amid the warm glow of polished wood. At the far end of the stylish room, a wall of windows offers an elevated view of the winery

floor, where stainless steel tanks gleam in sunlight shining through overhead windows, and barrels in the dim cellar area opposite rest in racks stacked to the ceiling. While sipping at the L-shaped bar, visitors can observe the Summerwood cellar staff at work.

Tasting room staffers receive extensive and ongoing training in all areas of the winery operation, including hands-on experience with pruning, harvesting, and even barrel washing. The breadth of their knowledge equips them to share detailed information about the wines and to ably answer even complex wine-related questions. Due to its central location among west side tasting rooms, the winery is often the first stop for travelers exploring wine country along Highway 46 West. Since staffers serve as regional ambassadors, they also keep current on the details of area hotels and restaurants, as well as hours and events at neighboring tasting rooms.

Summerwood was established in 2000 by the Fukae family of Osaka, Japan, and Mark Uhalley, a successful San Francisco–based businessman and wine enthusiast. The goal of the founders was to produce world-class wines, and they selected the property for its superb *terroir* and natural beauty. Their attention to detail shines through in the thoughtful remodeling of the original facility, as well as in the wine, which is made from both estate-grown grapes and fruit purchased from other west side vineyards, including Denner Vineyard and Halter Ranch Vineyard.

Offering a tranquil retreat and long pastoral views a mere ten minutes from downtown Paso Robles, the lushly landscaped winery and inviting tasting room rank among the west side's most celebrated destinations.

TABLAS CREEK VINEYARD

Truly a family affair, Tablas Creek Vineyard represents the culmination of two families' dreams to grow and make Rhône-style wines in California. In 1989 the Haas family, East Coast wine importers with fifty years of experience, partnered with the Perrins, proprietors of Châteauneuf du Pape's Château de Beaucastel since 1909, to establish an estate winery with vines sourced from the Perrins' renowned vineyard in France. Robert Haas first met the late Jacques Perrin in 1967 while in Europe scouting for vintages to import to his father's Manhattan wine shop. It took Perrin three years to agree to a deal, but so successful was the arrangement that, after Perrin's death, his sons named Haas their exclusive U.S. importer. The friendship between the families continued to grow and, twenty years later, led to their decision to start a winery from scratch.

The two families scoured the remote corners of California for a suitable site and purchased 120 acres on the west side of Paso Robles after spotting chalky outcroppings nearby that mimicked the limestone-based soils at Château de Beaucastel. They imported vine cuttings from Rhône varietals growing in the Perrins' vineyard in France, waited three years for them to clear the USDA-mandated quarantine, and finally began propagation in 1993.

Robert's son, Jason, a partner and general manager of Tablas Creek Vineyard, estimates that the nursery propagated two hundred thousand vines a year until moving off-site in 2004. It sold so many cuttings that Rhône-loving winemakers up and down the state began referring to the winery as "the mother ship." In 1997 the families harvested the first fruit from their organically farmed vineyard and, two years later, released their inaugural wines. Although the master plan did not initially include a tasting room, the partners soon realized that in a region famed for its Bordeaux-style wines, they needed to spread the word about Rhônes.

Opened in 2002, the tasting room sits amid a garden of roses, rosemary, and potted grapevines. Glass doors open onto a sheltered patio, and a vine-covered pergola provides a cool corridor to the main entry. To keep groups small and provide a more personal experience, the interior is divided into two rooms with a half-dozen tasting areas, some featuring views into the barrel room. The conversational buzz on a busy day sounds more like a living room full of friends than a retail space.

Winemaker Neil Collins ferments the wine using native yeasts, which impart characteristic flavors specific to the site. He carefully blends selected varietals and ages the wine primarily in twelve-hundred-gallon oak casks, just as the winemakers at Château de Beaucastel have done for a century.

TABLAS CREEK VINEYARD
9339 Adelaida Rd.
Paso Robles, CA 93446
805-237-1231
info@tablascreek.com
www.tablascreek.com

OWNERS: Haas and Perrin families.

LOCATION: 12 miles west of U.S. 101.

APPELLATION: Paso Robles.

HOURS: 10 A.M.–5 P.M. daily.

TASTINGS: $10 for 7–9 wines (applicable to wine purchases).

TOURS: 10:30 A.M. and 2 P.M. daily; appointments necessary, except on festival weekends.

THE WINES: Counoise, Grenache, Grenache Blanc, Marsanne, Mourvèdre, Picpoul Blanc, Roussanne, Syrah, Tannat, Viognier.

SPECIALTIES: Esprit de Beaucastel (Mourvèdre, Grenache, Syrah, Counoise blend), Esprit de Beaucastel Blanc (Roussanne, Grenache Blanc, Picpoul Blanc blend).

WINEMAKER: Neil Collins.

ANNUAL PRODUCTION: 18,000 cases.

OF SPECIAL NOTE: Wines are exclusively Rhône style. Tasting room sells oil made from on-site olive trees, as well as grapevines.

NEARBY ATTRACTION: Mt. Olive Organic Farm (tours, olive and olive oil tasting).

TOBIN JAMES CELLARS

TOBIN JAMES CELLARS
8950 Union Rd.
Paso Robles, CA 93446
805-239-2204
info@tobinjames.com
www.tobinjames.com

OWNERS: Tobin James, Lance and Claire Silver.

LOCATION: 9 miles east of downtown Paso Robles.

APPELLATION: Paso Robles.

HOURS: 10 A.M.–6 P.M. daily.

TASTINGS: Complimentary.

TOURS: None.

THE WINES: Barbera, Cabernet Franc, Cabernet Sauvignon, Chardonnay, Lagrein, Malbec, Merlot, Petit Verdot, Sangiovese, Sauvignon Blanc, sparkling wines, Syrah, Tempranillo, Zinfandel, dessert wines.

SPECIALTIES: Chateau Le Cacheflo (red blend), Estate Private Stash (Bordeaux blend), 5 (Bordeaux blend), Zinfandel.

WINEMAKERS: Tobin James, Lance Silver, Claire Silver, Jeff Poe.

ANNUAL PRODUCTION: 50,000 cases.

OF SPECIAL NOTE: Outdoor patio for picnicking. Free video games. Many limited-production wines sold in the tasting room only.

NEARBY ATTRACTIONS: Barney Schwartz Park (lake, picnic areas); Estrella Warbird Museum (restored military aircraft, memorabilia).

O n the eastern edge of the Paso Robles appellation stands a wine country outpost steeped in the worthy tradition of western hospitality. Built on the site of a nineteenth-century stagecoach stop, Tobin James Cellars welcomes guests into a tasting room reminiscent of a Gold Rush–era saloon, complete with a grand antique mahogany bar, opulent red wallpaper and lively music. Ceiling fans stir the air, while Victorian-style light fixtures illuminate a visual carnival of cowboy hats, large-format bottled wines, brass rails, lace curtains, and state fair ribbons. Origami dollar bills festoon an old-fashioned cash register, and two other tasting bars, built of matching mahogany, tell a tale of revelry.

Tobin James and his business partners, Lance and Claire Silver, want visitors to feel right at home, so they offer wine-friendly appetizers, wine samples, and family-friendly video games free of charge. In Claire Silver's view, the secret to the winery's overwhelming success lies in the owners' and staff's desire to give customers more than they expect.

Born in San Francisco, Tobin James was raised in Indiana, where his family's vineyard and wine-making activities caught his fancy at an early age. While working in his brother's Ohio wine shop, he met and received an offer to work crush from pioneering Paso Robles vintner Gary Eberle and, in 1980, happily headed west. Shumrick worked with Eberle for more than ten years, served as Peachy Canyon Winery's founding winemaker, and in 1994 built his own facility. Two years later, he formed a dynamic partnership with Lance and Claire Silver and in 2003 hired winemaker Jeff Poe to help handle the growing production at a winery that claims to observe only one rule: "have fun."

With an estate vineyard of just twenty acres, the partners must purchase most of their fruit, selecting red grapes primarily from local sources and whites from cooler regions in Arroyo Grande and Monterey County. The trio blends Zinfandel from forty different vineyards, including one that is eighty-five years old, and views the variety as a mighty spice rack from which to blend and create award-winning wines of remarkable depth and complexity.

After tasting, visitors who would like to enjoy some wine over a picnic lunch can head to the outdoor patio, a grotto of stone, brick, and glistening tile that easily qualifies as architectural art. From here, they can see the logo on the label mirrored in the distance as the glimmering sun sets over the wild, western hills of Paso Robles.

TOLO CELLARS

Tucked inside a grove of pine and ornamental plum trees just off Adelaida Road, the little red farmhouse that Tolo Cellars calls home casts an inviting silhouette against the blue backcountry sky. A rambling front yard and a wisteria-shaded patio frame the 1860s-era structure, giving it a homey, lived-in look, and the assorted outbuildings suggest a working ranch. Inside, owner/winemaker Josh Gibson has stocked the former living room with table linens, pottery, cookbooks, and gift items, leaving the brick-walled kitchen open for tasters. A 1930s-era gas range sits in one corner of the room, and against one wall is a nineteenth-century woodstove that belonged to the home's previous residents.

Gibson, who was born and raised in Paso Robles, likes the small-town feel of his vintage tasting room and can be found there most days pouring alongside one or two helpers. He enjoys meeting and mingling with his customers, and introducing them to his dog, Harley, a friendly half-pug, half-beagle breed called a puggle.

Gibson began his professional life in banking and stumbled into the world of winemaking in the late 1990s, when he recognized the name John Munch on a deposit slip and promptly asked his customer about wine. Munch, who founded Adelaida Cellars in 1981 and has since mentored dozens of winemakers, graciously answered all his questions. In 2000 Gibson took a job in the tasting room at Munch's current winery, Le Cuvier, while earning his MBA at Cal Poly San Luis Obispo. Crediting Munch as a gifted, natural teacher, Gibson began making wine as a side project a year later, while continuing to wear marketing, accounting, and sales hats at Le Cuvier.

Through trial, error, and spirited guidance from Munch, Gibson learned a "low-tech" approach to making wine, one that involves minimal intervention and no fining or filtering. He buys fruit from six vineyards lying within a seven-mile radius of the winery and relies on native yeasts to fuel his fermentations, citing his lack of formal training as the key to his success. He finds that the hardest part of winemaking is choosing names for the wines and has simply christened his blends with the lyrical names of Greek towns.

Gibson's family homesteaded in the Templeton area, and as a youth he traveled the Central Coast with his archaeologist father. He chose the name Tolo, a Chumash word meaning "mountain lion," because he wanted to link his winery with the land of his birth, its indigenous creatures, and the ancient hills that surround his little red farmhouse.

TOLO CELLARS
9750 Adelaida Rd.
Paso Robles, CA 93446
805-226-2282
josh@tolocellars.com
www.tolocellars.com

OWNER: Josh Gibson.

LOCATION: 12 miles west of U.S. 101.

APPELLATION: Paso Robles.

HOURS: 11 A.M.–5 P.M. Friday–Monday, and by appointment.

TASTINGS: $3 for 5 wines.

TOURS: None.

THE WINES: Cabernet Sauvignon, Chardonnay, Syrah, Zinfandel.

SPECIALTIES: Asíni (Sangiovese, Zinfandel blend), Léros (Syrah, Grenache, Mourvèdre, Counoise blend).

WINEMAKER: Josh Gibson.

ANNUAL PRODUCTION: 1,400 cases.

OF SPECIAL NOTE: Gift shop carries cookbooks, pottery, tablecloths, and Provençal linens. Tasting room is an 1860s-era farmhouse; fossils are visible in the chimney made of local stone.

NEARBY ATTRACTION: Mt. Olive Organic Farm (tours, olive and olive oil tasting).

TOLOSA WINERY

TOLOSA WINERY
4910 Edna Rd.
San Luis Obispo, CA 93401
805-782-0500
info@tolosawinery.com
www.tolosawinery.com

OWNERS: Bob Schiebelhut, Jim Efird, Robin Baggett.

LOCATION: Edna Valley, 4 miles southeast of downtown San Luis Obispo.

APPELLATION: Edna Valley.

HOURS: 11 A.M.–5 P.M. daily.

TASTINGS: $5 for 5 wines. $10 for 5 reserve wines; reservations recommended.

TOURS: Self-guided tours 11 A.M.–4:30 P.M. daily. Full facility tour with barrel tasting Monday–Friday by appointment ($30).

THE WINES: Chardonnay, Grenache, Petite Sirah, Pinot Gris, Pinot Noir, Sauvignon Blanc, Syrah, Viognier.

SPECIALTIES: Vineyard-designated Pinot Noir, Chardonnay, Syrah.

WINEMAKER: Larry Brooks.

ANNUAL PRODUCTION: 25,000 cases.

OF SPECIAL NOTE: Packaged deli snacks on-site. Food-and-wine pairings available 11 A.M.–3 P.M. ($15–$20) on weekends. Patio bar; picnic deck with fountain overlooking vineyards and crush pad. Educational sensory evaluation exhibit. Pinot Gris, Viognier, Sauvignon Blanc, Grenache, Rosé, Heritage Blend, and Petite Sirah available only in tasting room.

NEARBY ATTRACTIONS: Mission San Luis Obispo de Tolosa; San Luis Obispo County Historical Museum and other historic buildings in downtown San Luis Obispo; Pismo State Beach (swimming, hiking, camping).

In what is now the heart of historic downtown San Luis Obispo, the friars of Mission San Luis Obispo de Tolosa maintained a small vineyard, renowned throughout early California for its high-quality wines. Tolosa Winery's name honors the role of the mission in starting the region's wine industry, and the winery aims to achieve a similar reputation for crafting some of the finest wines in the state.

Tolosa Winery is the brainchild of Bob Schiebelhut, an attorney and self-trained winemaker who moved to the area in 1978 to start a law practice. A decade later, he approached pioneering viticulturalist Jim Efird and his law partner, Robin Baggett, with the idea of starting an estate vineyard and eventually building a first-rate facility in which to make premium wines. Efird, from a farming family near Fresno, had relocated to San Luis Obispo to plant Para- gon Vineyards in 1973—a time when garbanzo beans and grain covered much of the region's farmland. Over the next thirty years, Efird helped plant most of the vineyards on the coastal hills of southern San Luis Obispo.

The Tolosa group acquired mineral-rich property near Islay Hill, an ancient volcanic plug just south of the San Luis Obispo Airport. They divided the 720 acres into five separate vineyards and began planting grapevines in 1992. Half of the vineyards are planted to Chardonnay; another 40 percent are devoted to Pinot Noir; and the remainder includes small amounts of Syrah, Sauvignon Blanc, Pinot Gris, Grenache, Viognier, and Petite Sirah. At first Tolosa sold fruit to local winemakers. As the sustainably farmed vineyards matured, they began to keep the top 10 percent of the harvest for themselves. Consultant and noted winemaker Larry Brooks, an expert in transforming San Luis Obispo County fruit into top-flight wines, came to Tolosa in 2000 to direct winemaking in a state-of-the-art facility amid the vineyards. In 2001 Tolosa Winery released its first vintages, and the brand soon earned widespread accolades for its elegant character and reflection of the Edna Valley *terroir*.

The award-winning design of the tasting room reflects elements used in winemaking: stainless steel, cork, glass, and wood. Fiber-optic lights shine seven alternating colors on the built-in birch shelves behind the curved, glass-topped tasting bar. Guests can educate themselves about wine by inhaling different wine aromas at a granite sensory evaluation station. The visitor area flows outdoors onto a spacious patio with an abstract fountain overlooking the gardens, covered with lavender, olive trees, iris, and the vineyards inspired by their predecessor at Mission San Luis Obispo de Tolosa.

TOLOSA
"1772"

Varietal:	*Pinot Noir*
Appellation:	*Edna Valley*
Vineyard:	*Edna Ranch*
Vintage:	*2006*
Bottles Produced:	*6,268*
Blocks:	*596, 597, 595*
TA: *6.68* pH: *3.54* Brix: *23.9˚: 25.6˚*	
Alcohol by Vol.: *13.8%*	
Bottle Number:	

Vina Robles

A red-roofed showplace that draws visitors from around the world, the Vina Robles hospitality center opened in 2007, ten years after its owner, Swiss entrepreneur Hans Nef, planted his three estate vineyards on Paso Robles's east side. Nef built the winery and center with a variety of events in mind—from barbecues and concerts to banquets and conferences—and created a wonderfully functional complex of terraces, courtyards, and indoor spaces. Pillars and thick walls composed of carefully fitted stones lend dramatic mass to the structures and reflect an architectural style inspired by California's sunny climate and Franciscan missions. A large arbor supported by stone columns joins two heritage oaks in shading the entryway, as soft music drifts about the courtyard and blends with the sound of water splashing in nearby fountains.

Inside, visitors can wander through the gift shop stocked with locally made items, kitchenware, crystal glasses, and gourmet goodies, before heading into the impressive tasting area. Just past the exposed stone walls of the foyer, a massive fireplace promises winter warmth, paintings made of brilliant pigments baked onto stainless steel hang be- low a row of lofty windows, and a sheer sense of space prevails. In front of a huge, arched window that looks over the demonstration vine-

yard, stacked glassware glints from behind the triangular concrete bar. Here, wine aficionados can enjoy complimentary samples of nonreserve vintages or pay a nominal fee to sip the Cuvée Collection of signature blends. Daring visitors might want to try a Vina Tini—a dry rosé swizzled with apple martini mix—or a flute of sparkling wine sweetened with a splash of local grape juice.

Marc Laderriere, vice president of sales and marketing, explains that although the winery is not European, its principals do embrace a "European approach" that favors wines with modest alcohol content and a distinctive, bright finish. To create those wines, in 1999 Nef hired winemaker Matthias Gubler, who was born in Switzerland and is experienced in both French and Californian enological traditions. Gubler and Nef, who share a national heritage and native tongues, communicate effectively in English, German, and Swiss-German to realize their common goals in the cellar.

In addition to wine tasting, the hospitality center hosts a variety of innovative events, including a series showcasing the region's finest food, music, and handicrafts; rotating art exhibits in the courtyard; and summer concerts on the lawn. Each week, a professional instructor teaches ballroom dancing, from tango to swing, followed by a social hour of wine and light appetizers, all part of the fun on Paso Robles's east side.

Vina Robles
3700 Mill Rd.
Paso Robles, CA 93446
805-227-4812
info@vinarobles.com
www.vinarobles.com

Owner: Hans Nef.

Location: 3 miles east of Hwy. 46 East.

Appellation: Paso Robles.

Hours: 10 a.m.–5 p.m. daily in winter; 10 a.m.–6 p.m. daily in summer.

Tastings: Complimentary; $5 for 3 wines from the Cuvée Collection.

Tours: None.

The Wines: Cabernet Sauvignon, Petit Verdot, Petite Sirah, Sauvignon Blanc, Syrah, Viognier, Zinfandel.

Specialties: Signature (Petit Verdot, Cabernet Sauvignon, Syrah blend), Suendero (Cabernet Sauvignon, Petit Verdot blend), Syrée (Syrah, Petite Sirah, Cabernet Sauvignon blend).

Winemaker: Matthias Gubler.

Annual Production: 25,000 cases.

Of Special Note: Cheese-and-wine pairings offered daily ($10). Gift shop featuring Dean & Deluca gourmet foods and cookbooks. Deli section with artisan cheeses and meats. Terrace, patio, and lawn areas for picnicking. Art exhibit on display. On-going events (concerts, art shows, ballroom dancing). Self-guided tours of demonstration vineyard.

Nearby Attractions: Barney Schwartz Park (lake, picnic areas); Paso Robles City Park (site of festivals, summer concerts, farmers market).

WHALEBONE VINEYARD

WHALEBONE VINEYARD
8325 Vineyard Dr.
Paso Robles, CA 93446
805-239-9020
jan@whalebonevineyard.
com
www.whalebonevineyard.
com

OWNERS: Bob and Janalyn
Simpson.

LOCATION: 8 miles north-
west of intersection of
Hwy. 46 West and
Vineyard Dr.

APPELLATION: Paso Robles.

HOURS: 11 A.M.–5 P.M.
Monday–Thursday;
11 A.M.–5:30 P.M. Friday–
Sunday.

TASTINGS: $5 for 5 wines
(applicable to purchase).

TOURS: None.

THE WINES: Cabernet Sauvignon, Syrah, Zinfandel.

SPECIALTY: Bob Wine
(Cabernet Sauvignon
blend).

WINEMAKER: Dan Kleck.

ANNUAL PRODUCTION:
2,500 cases.

OF SPECIAL NOTE: Winery
serves signature barbecue
tri-tip "sliders" with bal-
samic glaze, free of charge,
during major wine country
events.

NEARBY ATTRACTION:
Mt. Olive Organic Farm
(tours, olive and olive oil
tasting).

Sitting on an island of grass, the Whalebone Vineyard tasting room resembles an old hay barn, except for the harpoons jutting from the roof extensions. A patio with shaded tables flanks one side, and a boulder bearing fossilized whalebones indicates the long-ago presence of a salty sea. Whalebone Vineyard lies just eight miles from the Pacific Ocean, and when owners Bob and Janalyn Simpson planted their fossil-studded vineyard in 1989, they eagerly adopted the nautical theme. For their label, they even chose a font that incorporates a tiny harpoon into each letter.

New in 2007, the tasting room was built with Jefferson pine salvaged from an 1880s-era barn. Inside, wire-brushed walls flecked 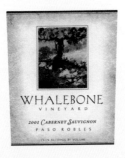 with nail holes hold a gallery of family photos, including one crowded collage of babies delivered by Bob, a retired obstetrician. Stamped copper covers the front of the mesquite tasting bar, and shelves hold tie-dyed shirts and hand towels sewn by Janalyn. An Iowa farm girl, Janalyn joins her daughter, and occasionally her sister, in welcoming visitors to the tasting room as if they were family members entering her living room. Though Bob pops in occasionally, he's usually busy maintaining the couple's twenty-six head of cattle and dry-farmed ten-acre vineyard planted to Cabernet Sauvignon. At eighteen hundred feet in elevation, the south-facing vineyard is prone to deep temperature drops and often holds its fruit well into November for a remarkable concentration of flavors.

The Simpsons bought their 128-acre property in 1986 from the estate of film director King Vidor. The couple raised horses and cattle, until "the romance of the vineyard" enticed them to farm grapes for area winemakers. In 1994 the Simpsons set aside some fruit, and a friend created the iconic Bob Wine, a Cabernet Sauvignon–based blend. The wine won medals and fans, and led to their first commercial release in 2001. A year later, the pair hired the accomplished Dan Kleck as winemaker, and though they no longer sell fruit, they do buy local Zinfandel and Syrah.

According to local theory, Mammoth Mountain, nearly two hundred miles northeast, erupted thirty million years ago, emitting clouds of ash that smothered and preserved some five thousand whales swimming in a shallow sea. A series of earthquakes uplifted the seabed to form both the Coastal Range and the perfect soil for growing Cabernet Sauvignon, the Simpsons' favorite grape.

WILD HORSE WINERY

One of the oldest producers in the region, Wild Horse Winery completed its first crush in 1983, the year that Paso Robles became an official appellation. Named for the wild mustangs that once roamed the neighboring hills, it remains a local favorite, renowned for its eclectic portfolio of wines, prolific organic vegetable garden, and Floyd, the resident llama.

Founder Ken Volk chose the east side of Paso Robles for his vineyard because of its low-vigor soils, believing their lean constitution would force his sustainably farmed vineyard to produce grapes with highly concentrated flavors. An ambitious experimenter, he planted forty-five acres with thirty-three varietals, some of them considered unusual even by today's standards. Among the blocks of Chardonnay and Cabernet Sauvignon, he included heirlooms like Verdelho, Blaufränkisch, Negrette, and Malvasia Bianca, from which the winery still produces tasting-room-exclusive vintages. Vineyard workers continue to employ the sustainable methods pioneered by Volk. They brew compost tea to feed the vines, use a state-of-the-art water recycling system, and compost the pomace left behind by the grape presses. Sheep are used for weed control and are protected from coyotes by Floyd.

The winery and tasting room lie at the end of a long road, past two ranch-style gates and a vineyard edged with alternating red and white rosebushes. A wooden pergola, a garden, and a picnic patio mark the entrance to the tasting room, where visitors can sample from equine-themed lists, such as the Four Horseman and Unbridled Flight. If hunger strikes, they can enhance the experience with packaged pairings of cheese, nuts, crackers, and sweets. Horses inform the décor and inventory of the room: a framed photo of wild mustangs mirrors the winery's logo horse as it gallops across hats, T-shirts, and rows of wine bottles. Display tables offer a diverse assortment of books, crystal glassware, wine accessories, jams, nut brittle, and local olive oil.

Today, the estate vineyard provides about 4 percent of the fruit needed to fuel the facility's extensive varietal program, so every fall winemakers Clay Brock and Chrissy Wittmann select from grapes grown in more than forty Central Coast vineyards, some of which have been supplying the winery since its inception. As a tribute to the name that Volk chose twenty-five years ago, the winery makes an annual donation to Return to Freedom, a regional equine sanctuary, where herds of wild horses still roam California's hills.

WILD HORSE WINERY
1437 Wild Horse
Winery Ct.
Templeton, CA 93465
805-434-2541
leslie.churchill@
iconestateswine.com
www.wildhorsewinery.
com

OWNER: Icon Estates.

LOCATION: 10 miles south of downtown Paso Robles.

APPELLATION: Paso Robles.

HOURS: 11 A.M.–5 P.M. daily.

TASTINGS: $5 for 5 wines; $10 for 5 reserve wines.

TOURS: None.

THE WINES: Barbera, Blaufränkisch, Cabernet Sauvignon, Chardonnay, Malvasia Bianca, Merlot, Negrette, Pinot Noir, Verdelho, Viognier.

SPECIALTIES: Cheval Sauvage (Pinot Noir), Unbridled (Chardonnay, Merlot, Cabernet Sauvignon, Zinfandel blend).

WINEMAKERS: Clay Brock, Chrissy Wittmann.

ANNUAL PRODUCTION: 200,000 cases.

OF SPECIAL NOTE: Patio for picnicking. Gift shop featuring local olive oil, wine accessories, and other items. Free organic produce in season. Heirloom and Unbridled wines available only in tasting room.

NEARBY ATTRACTIONS: Templeton Park (events including weekly summer concerts); Jack Creek Farms (demonstration gardens, pick-your-own produce, May–November).

WINDWARD VINEYARD

WINDWARD VINEYARD
1380 Live Oak Rd.
Paso Robles, CA 93446
805-239-2565
maggie@windward
vineyard.com
www.windwardvineyard.
com

OWNERS: Marc Goldberg,
Maggie D'Ambrosia.

LOCATION: 1 mile west of
U.S. 101.

APPELLATION: Paso Robles.

HOURS: 10:30 A.M.–5 P.M.
daily.

TASTINGS: $10 for 4 wines.

TOURS: By appointment.

THE WINE: Pinot Noir.

SPECIALTY: Estate-grown
Burgundian-style Pinot
Noir.

WINEMAKER:
Marc Goldberg.

ANNUAL PRODUCTION:
2,000 cases.

OF SPECIAL NOTE: Ivy-
covered lath house with
vineyard view for pic-
nicking. Artisan cheeses
available for purchase.
Nearly all the wine is sold
exclusively through tasting
room.

NEARBY ATTRACTION:
Paso Robles City Park
(site of festivals, summer
concerts, farmers market).

True vignerons, Windward Vineyard's Marc Goldberg and Maggie D'Ambrosia make wine according to the Burgundian model of "monopole": maintaining complete control over their vines, vinifying only estate fruit, and never selling a single grape. In their fifteen-acre vineyard, planted exclusively to Pinot Noir, the duo grows four clones chosen specifically to allow the vineyard "to speak about itself in the glass." Goldberg doesn't fine, filter, or acidulate the wine, a minimalist approach that he feels lets the signature qualities of each vineyard block shine through. The couple releases two wines a year—  Monopole and Gold Barrel Select—each featuring honeyed notes of wild strawberries and Bing cherries, and what Goldberg calls "the Windward peacock-tail finish," a fanning out of complex flavors dusted with a touch of oak. In 2008, after nearly twenty years of meticu-lous winemaking, Goldberg and D'Ambrosia were named San Luis Obispo County's Winemakers of the Year at the Cental Coast Wine Classic.

Goldberg, who describes his first sip of Pinot Noir at age seventeen as "magic," makes wine in a traditional style that benefits from twenty years or more of cellaring. He marvels at the fifteen hundred years that it took for Pinot Noir to become Burgundy's king, and regards his own role not as that of a technician but as a "wine shepherd" charged with protecting the integrity of his grapes.

In the late 1980s, over a glass of Champagne, Goldberg met D'Ambrosia, his future wife and business partner, in his hometown of Pittsburgh, Pennsylvania. Both were hospital administrators, and as they relocated as necessary for their jobs, they eventually crossed the country, tasting Pinot Noir along the way. The pair preferred nuanced French vintages to the denser New World offerings, until they sampled a 1976 Hoffman Mountain Ranch Pinot Noir from a vineyard five miles west of Paso Robles. Struck by the balance and beauty of the wine, they embraced the grand challenge of making Burgundian-style Pinot Noir in the United States.

Inspired by the work of Dr. Hoffman and the legendary enologist André Tchelistcheff, who in the late 1960s planted some of the west side's first Pinot Noir, the couple bought a barley farm in the Templeton Gap region west of Paso Robles. They planted their vineyard in 1989, on land bearing conditions similar to those of Hoffman's ranch nearby, and released their first wine in 1993.

Visitors to Windward Vineyard's art-filled tasting room find an atmosphere of cool elegance amid the rural quiet. Tucked behind an ivy-draped lath house (where lingering is encouraged), the combination winery/tasting room offers a view of the barrel room and an ideal setting for discover-ing the magic of Pinot Noir.

Wine House Press
127 East Napa Street, Suite F
Sonoma, CA 95476
707-996-1741

Editor and publisher: Tom Silberkleit
Original design: Jennifer Barry Design
Production: Poulson Gluck Design
Copyeditor: Judith Dunham
Cartographer: Ben Pease
Artistic development: Lisa Silberkleit
Proofreader: Linda Bouchard

All photographs by Robert Holmes, except the following:
page 74, Ron Bez Photography; page 130, bottom left, Deborah Denker Photography.

Front cover photograph: Opolo Vineyards, Paso Robles
Back cover photographs: top left: Maloy O'Neill Vineyards;
top right: Cambria Estate Winery; bottom left: Anglim Winery; bottom right: Tolo Cellars

"The Etiquette of Wine Tasting" and "Reading a Wine Label" essays: Marty Olmstead

Printed and bound in Singapore through DNP America, LLC
ISBN-13: 978-0-9724993-0-9

First Edition

Distributed by Ten Speed Press, P.O. Box 7123, Berkeley, CA 94707, www.tenspeed.com

The publisher has made every effort to ensure the accuracy of the information contained in
The California Directory of Fine Wineries, but can accept no liability for any loss, injury, or inconvenience
sustained by any visitor as a result of any information or recommendation contained in this guide.
Travelers should always call ahead to confirm hours of operation, fees, and other highly variable information.

Always act responsibly when drinking alcoholic beverages by selecting a designated driver or prearranged transportation.

Customized Editions
Wine House Press will print custom editions of this volume for bulk purchase at your request. Personalized covers and
foil-stamped corporate logo imprints can be created in large quantities for special promotions or events, or as premiums.
For more information, contact Custom Imprints, Wine House Press, 127 E. Napa Street, Suite F, Sonoma, CA 95476; 707-996-1741.

OTHER BOOKS BY WINE HOUSE PRESS

The California Directory of Fine Wineries — Northern Region
Napa • Sonoma • Mendocino

Acknowledgments

Creativity, perseverance, integrity, and commitment are fundamental qualities for guaranteeing the success of a project. The artistic and editorial teams who worked on this edition possess these qualities in large measures. My heartfelt thanks go to K. Reka Badger and Cheryl Crabtree, writers; Robert Holmes, photographer; Judith Dunham, copyeditor; Linda Bouchard, proofreader; Poulson Gluck Design, production; and Ben Pease, cartographer.

In addition, I am grateful for the invaluable counsel and encouragement of Chester and Frances Arnold; Danny Biederman; Annette Burden; Chrystal Clifton; Fran Clow; Kris Curran; Jenny Williamson Doré; Matt Duggan and the team at *Wine Country* in Los Olivos, California; Brett Escalera; Jim Fiolek; Stacie Jacob; my esteemed parents—Estelle Silberkleit and William Silberkleit; Joan Tapper; Christopher Taranto; and the scores of readers and winery enthusiasts who have contacted me to say how much they enjoy this book series.

I also extend my deepest appreciation to Victor Popp and the staff of La Quinta Inn and Suites of Paso Robles, California, for their hospitality and enthusiastic support of this project. Special thanks as well go to Maurice Boyd of Fess Parker's Santa Barbara County Wine Center for lending critical logistic assistance. And finally, for her love and creative input, as well as for enduring work-filled weekends and midnight deadlines, my gratitude and affection go to Lisa Silberkleit.

— Tom Silberkleit